MW00632429

REND THE HEAVENS

STORIES OF AWAKENING

FRANK DI PIETRO

Christos

Rend The Heavens: Stories of Awakening
by Frank Di Pietro
Copyright © 2022

Christos Publishing
Post Office Box 1333
Lees Summit, MO 64063

First Printing, in the United States, March 2022.
For Worldwide Distribution
All rights reserved.
ISBN: 978-1-950053-36-0

For other exciting releases from Christos Publishing visit our store:
www.TheResurgenceStore.com

Cover design by Shawn Jonas | sjonas@wrckc.com

*Christos Publishing produces superbly researched Christian books informed by a Spirit-led
worldview.*

"Oh, that you would rend the heavens and come down, that the mountains would tremble before you!

As when fire sets twigs ablaze and causes water to boil, come down to make your name known to your enemies and cause the nations to quake before you!

For when you did awesome things that we did not expect, you came down, and the mountains trembled before you.

Since ancient times no one has heard, no ear has perceived, no eye has seen any God besides you, who acts on behalf of those who wait for him."

—Isaiah 64:1-4 NIV

I dedicate this book to my wife, Melissa. She has not only been a loving companion over the years, but she was also tenacious enough to pray this stone-cold heart into the Kingdom of God.

This work also goes out to my good friend, J. D. King. I am grateful for his encouragement and friendly nudging. It's what I needed to get this book completed.

Finally, I want to dedicate this work to all the Christian witnesses, over the centuries, who proved through their lives that Jesus is worthy of all honor and praise!

CONTENTS

FOREWORD

COREY RUSSELL

"Thus says the High and Lofty One who inhabits eternity, whose name *is* Holy: 'I dwell in the high and holy *place,* with him *who* has a contrite and humble spirit, to revive the spirit of the humble, and to revive the heart of the contrite ones'" (Isaiah 57:15 NKJV).

I believe that the Body of Christ in the United States of America has lost a sense of the holiness and sacredness of revival. Many believers have forgotten what it means.

I see so many on social media using this word to describe what is happening through their ministries. While I'm grateful to God for every person touched, every body healed, and every thing restored, I'm also aware that we have fallen far from the biblical and historical reality of what revival truly is.

This is why I'm so grateful for Frank Di Pietro's new book, *Rend the Heavens: Stories of Awakening*. In this inspiring collection, Di Pietro calls on believers to look to the past—seeing what revival has looked like—to reframe our expectations for both the present and future.

My prayer is that through this book God, would light your heart on fire with a deep burden to see revival touch this generation like never before.

—Corey Russell
Author and Speaker
www.coreyrussell.org

INTRODUCTION

"Will You not revive us again so that Your people may rejoice in you?" (Psalm 85:6).

It delights me to delve into the old stories of revival. When one ponders how God affected lives in preceding generations, it positions them to have a fresh encounter.

Every revival is unique, but there are commonalities that each one of them shares. When we recognize the patterns, it helps us find the signs of grace in our era.

This volume is called *Rend The Heavens: Stories of Awakening*. This title comes from the prayer of the prophet Isaiah. Centuries ago, he declared,

"Oh, that You would rend the heavens! That You would come down! That the mountains might shake at Your presence" (Isaiah 64:1 NKJV).

In the mid-Twentieth Century, Donald John Smith drew upon this verse as he interceded for revival in the Hebrides Islands. The fervent proclamation of this verse precipitated a mighty move of God.

We're in an era where we need God to rend the heavens once more. The church needs to be reawakened and brought back to the majesty of Jesus. If we don't encounter a fresh outpouring of the Holy Spirit, the next generation may be lost.

May the succeeding stories of awakening provoke you to intercede and cry out to God. Something glorious awaits those who labor and pray for the glory of the Lord in our generation.

—Frank "J. J." DiPietro

PROLOGUE

"O LORD, I have heard the report of you, and your work, O LORD, do I fear. In the midst of the years revive it; in the midst of the years make it known; in wrath remember mercy" (Habakkuk 3:2 ESV).

~

I spend every morning reflecting on the Word of God. Recently, the opening chapters of Joshua struck me. You probably already know this story, but Israel was struggling on the edge of the Promised Land. Then the Lord stopped the flow of the Jordan River and compelled them to step over into their inheritance.

As they advanced, the Lord asked Israel to pull twelve stones from the riverbed. They were to pile these stones together. This was a memorial for the next generation.

Joshua said to the Israelites, "In the future when your descendants ask their fathers, 'What do these stones mean?' tell

them, 'Israel crossed the Jordan on dry ground'" (Joshua
4:21-22).

The stones helped them commemorate the stories of
deliverance and breakthrough. They brought a sense of awe and
wonder every time Israel came upon them.

But over time, God's people have a habit of overlooking the
stones. Our kids stop asking questions, and the fathers'
testimonies are forgotten.

A nation who loses sight of their heritage probably will not be
in a position to counteract the darkness that invariably appears.

We must go back to what brings glory and wonder. When
stones of remembrance are rediscovered, we not only see the
heart of God, but inheritances are reapprehended. The old
accounts stir Christians to experience new awakenings.

I wrote this book to be a "stone of remembrance"—a
reminder of the glory that our mothers and fathers knew. I hope
that *Rend The Heavens* will stir your heart and empower you as
you embrace your glorious destiny.

It is time to cry out to God!

—Frank "J. J." DiPietro

REND THE HEAVENS

GERHARD TERSTEEGEN

Gerhard Tersteegen

"I never prayed sincerely and earnestly for anything, but it came at some time; no matter at how distant a day, somehow, in some shape...it came." —Adoniram Judson

"Jesus Christ carries on intercession for us in heaven; The Holy Ghost carries on intercession in us on the earth; and we the saints have to carry on intercession for all men." —Oswald Chambers

"The church has not yet touched the fringe of the possibility of intercessory prayer. Her largest victories will be witnessed when individual Christians everywhere come to recognize their priesthood unto God and day by day give themselves unto prayer." —John R. Mott

"God has no greater controversy with His people than this, that with boundless promises to believing prayer, there are so few who actually give themselves to intercession." —A. T. Pierson

"I used to think that prayer should have the first place and teaching the second. I now feel that it would be truer to give prayer the first, second, and third place, and teaching fourth."—James O. Fraser

When the name Gerhard Tersteegen is mentioned in revivalist circles, they remember him as a firebrand set apart for God. His fervor and devotion were legendary. This German intercessor loved Mark 12:30, which affirms: "You shall love the Lord your God with all your heart, with all your soul, and with all your mind and with all your strength" (Mark 12:30). Reflecting on this passage, Tersteegan once said,

"O that I might be no more, nor have any longer in myself either life, or understanding, or will, or thought, or any other motion, and that Thou, my God, my Jesus, might be and work all in me . . . Condemn and destroy in me all which Thou art not and which is not Thee. Take entire possession...and do in me and through me what is pleasing in Thy sight. Let me exist no more but Thou alone be all in all."

This German intercessor spent his life pursuing intimate fellowship with God. A man knew him once remarked: "When he prayed, it was as if he went straight into heaven and lost himself in God, and usually when he was done praying, he was as white as the wall."

Daily, Tersteegen spent most of his waking hours before the throne of God. He was in such constant intercession that a heavenly presence rested over his home and the surrounding area. A tavern owner who regularly passed his home said,

"When I pass by that man's house, a great awe comes over me of some holy presence. And when I think about him, it has more power over me than many a sermon."

When Tersteegen interceded, he often received what he asked for. He once said,

"Prayer is simply asking God to do for us what he has promised us He will do if we ask Him...asking is man's part. Giving is God's part. The praying belongs to us. The answer belongs to God."

Beginning in his youth, the intercessor sought God. He strived to imitate Christ in every realm of existence. Jesus is the image of the invisible God (Colossians 1:15), and every believer is called to be the visible image of the invisible Jesus. The scripture that declares, "Be Holy as I am Holy" (1 Peter 1:16) always struck him.

Prayers like the following were continually being uttered by this godly man:

"How willingly would I be freed from the bondage of lusts and
of empty pleasure, but I find no strength or capability for it. This
cannot be until the Lord Himself revels Himself in us, raises up
His dwelling place in us, and inhabits it, filling it with His life,
so that we are clothed in Him, and He Himself thus fulfills in us
all the righteousness of the Law."

While contemplating the meaning of devotion, this
passionate intercessor went deep into realms of glory. He
embraced a life of self-surrender and scriptural immersion.
Colleagues called him a mystic—impressed with his insights into
the mysteries of heaven. But Tersteegen was not bizarre. He was
adamant that spirituality should always be centered in Christ.
The intercessor said, "Faith is . . . a dwelling of Christ in the
soul, and of the soul in Christ, and a becoming one with Him."

Continually searching for avenues to commune with God,
Tersteegen's calling was not to be an evangelist, pastor, or
missionary. He wasn't even called to be the leader of an earth-
shaking revival. His mandate was to be a model of prayer—one
who helped solidify faith in the hearts of men.

This German prayer warrior modeled the compassion and
mercy of Jesus everywhere he went. He was fixated on God's love
and encouraged others to encounter it as well. He clarified that
one didn't have to die to encounter God's glory. It was something
that could be experienced now if one would only surrender to the
Lord.

Tersteegen liked to say, "Taste and see how gracious the Lord
is, and how unspeakably blessed we may be in communion with
Him, even during the present state of existence!"

BEGINNINGS

Gerhard Tersteegen was born on November 25, 1697 in Mors,
Germany and baptized on January 12, 1698. He was the second

youngest of eight children. His father, Henricus, was a pious member of the Reformed Church and died when Gerhard was six years of age. His mother, Conera, managed to pull some strings and send him to the elite Adolfinum Grammer School that emphasized learning foreign languages. The Heidelberg Catechism was taught in Latin and German, and scripture was studied in Hebrew and Greek.

On leaving the school, he was a skilled linguist, trained in French, Dutch, German, Latin, Hebrew, and Greek. But instead of furthering his education, he became a merchant, earning his living in textiles.

During this time, Tersteegen sought to have a deep spiritual encounter with God. He withdrew from everything, living on one scanty meal a day. He rejected coffee, tea, and all other luxuries. His problem was he was trying to meet God in his own strength. These fruitless efforts led him to a deep depression, and he became too weak to work.

This broken man realized the ways he was taught to enter into holiness were virtually impossible. In his struggle to overcome the world, and his flesh, he was denying too much of the grace and mercy of God.

Surrendering his heart and mind to kindness of the Lord, Tersteegen experienced heavenly love like he never encountered before. He wrote,

> "The secret of God's presence is actually believed by very few, but are you aware, that if each one truly believed it, the whole world would at once be filled with the saints, and the earth would be truly Paradise."

This German supplicant desired a Christ-filled life. So, every day, he spent hours in prayer and scripture reading. His dullness was soon replaced with "a spiritual sight of the Sun of Righteousness with healing in His wings."

TOUCHING THE LIVES OF OTHERS

Relishing in the overflow of mercy, Tersteegen began sharing messages about the Bible in various parts of the city. He became known for deeply spiritual sermons that cut listeners to the heart. People crowded into his home to hear him speak of the mighty things of God. When there was no more room in the house, some brought ladders to scale the wall and hear the words of this powerful intercessor through the upper windows.

Tersteegen wanted everyone to encounter the Lord. Focusing on the importance of the Baptism in the Holy Spirit, he once said,

> "When the Spirit enters into the heart, He fills it entirely, so that the world finds no more room or place for it, because this quest makes Himself sole Lord and Master of it."

Between 1725-1727, he led a great awakening that took place in the Ruhr District. This part of the city soon became known as "Tersteegen Territory," as thousands gathered to hear him preach in open-air meetings. Three Reformed pastors in that region protested and demanded his arrest. However, the mayor was a friend of the revival and refused to take action. Tersteegen ultimately urged the opposing ministers to join the revival. They agreed and soon their churches were full of worshippers, too.

Many sought Tersteegen's wisdom and council. As many as thirty people gathered in his parlor every evening. Multitudes traveled to hear him preach. King Frederick the Great, heard of his godly wisdom and summoned him to the palace to talk about God. The intercessor's advice was simple and to the point. He declared to the monarch:

> "You are the child of God. God's nature is in you. It has only become overclouded. Withdraw from outward things. Pray, and

you will make contact again with God, the source of your being. Forget yourself. Forget your selfish desires. Look to God. Die to your own will, live for God's will and you will know true life."

CONTROVERSIES

Tersteegen was unique in his willingness to celebrate the work of the Spirit within the various religious traditions. He thought it was foolish to believe any one group had sole access to God. He believed faithful witnesses were evident in every Christian denomination—including the Roman Catholic Church.

The intercessor incited outrage in Protestant circles when he wrote a two-volume collection of biographical sketches, celebrating devout Catholic saints. Some felt this was over the line, and some of his friends turned against him.

Another difficulty arose when government officials began cracking down on "unauthorized preachers." A law was passed on June 28, 1740, that forbade anyone from ministering except ordained Roman Catholic, Lutheran, and Reformed ministers. Not identifying with any of those traditions, Tersteegen was considered a "nonconformist." Thus, he was not allowed to preach in a public meeting for a decade. However, nothing could keep this man of God silent.

REVIVAL

Because of Tersteegen's impassioned preaching, a powerful revival sparked in Holland and its flames spread to Germany in 1750. As the awakening grew, and Tersteegen's preaching was more widely recognized, opposing pastors appealed to the courts to uphold the law that prohibited unauthorized preaching. The opposition made their case, but the judges refused to comply. The masses supported the revival, and the will of the people triumphed over the antagonists.

Both the wealthy and poor citizens of Mulheim gathered outside the intercessor's house to hear him preach through an open window. From sunrise to sunset, he expounded the scriptures and revealed the mysteries of Jesus. This fervent revival continued until the beginning of the *Seven Years War*.

Because Mulheim became the epicenter of conflict, it became dangerous. Friends urged Tersteegen to flee to Holland, but he refused to leave. The great preacher became even more unrelenting in his gospel proclamation. Crowds came from miles around to hear his words as he preached, day and night. Eventually, this intense labor took a toll on his health. Although his spirit remained strong, his body was broken.

LAST WILL AND TESTAMENT

In the aftermath of this challenging era, Tersteegen's body was wracked by strained breathing and severe coughing. Eventually his kidneys failed and gout set in, along with a debilitating hernia. Amid the crippling pain, he continued to preach from his bed to all who gathered to hear him.

Tersteegen wrote his last will and testament like a sermon. In it, he gave away his earthly possessions and thanked God for His mercies. He ended this document with the following declaration:

> "In childlike humble trust in the divine mercy of Christ, I now trust in and await that when my eyes close and others pronounce me dead, I shall at last enter into eternal life and be forever with my Lord."

Toward the end, Tersteegen's pains increased as he experienced severe swelling and convulsions. But he would not let up. He still preached as a steady stream of visitors passed by his couch to hear a last word or overhear the praise that was continually on his lips. He once said,

"My sentiments and my religion are these, that as one who is reconciled to God, through the blood of Christ, I suffer the Spirit of Jesus, by means of mortification, affliction, and prayer, to lead me away from self, and all created good, in order that I may live safely to God in Christ Jesus; and cleaving by faith and love to Him, I hope to become one spirit with Him, and through His mercy in Christ alone, to obtain eternal felicity."

On April 3, 1769, at two o'clock in the morning, Tersteegen said, "Oh Jesus, sweet Jesus." Then he closed his eyes and looked upon the face of the One whose life he imitated.

Gerhard Tersteegen, through intercession and devotion of Jesus, impacted an entire generation. His godly influence continued to inspire seekers long after his death. He authored several books and a poetry collection on the glory of God. Tersteegen also wrote 111 hymns, publishing them in a collection called, "A Spiritual Flower Garden for Ardent Souls."

Tersteegen, through his writing, life, and intercession, modeled what it meant to be wholly devoted to Christ. Though he is dead, his example lives on.

"That I may know Him and the power of His resurrection, and the fellowship of His sufferings, being conformed to His death, if by any means, I may attain to the resurrection from the dead" (Philippians 3:10-11).

2

GEORGE WHITEFIELD

George Whitefield

"A dead ministry will always make a dead people, whereas of
ministers who are warmed with the love of God themselves,

they cannot but be instruments of diffusing that love among others."—George Whitefield

"Men who long ago lost their anointing still minister, using the same clichés and mannerisms. But they are not feared in hell; they are just 'clouds without water.' Lord, have mercy."— Leonard Ravenhill

"And as the circumcision in the flesh, and not the heart, have no part in God's good promises, even so they that are baptized in the flesh, and not in the heart have no place in Christ's blood." —William Booth

"And now let me address all of you, high and low, rich and poor, one with another, to accept of mercy and grace while it is offered to you. Now is the accepted time, now is the day of salvation, and will you not accept it, now it is offered unto you?"—George Whitefield

The English colonies were entering a desperate time with the dawning of the eighteenth century. The church had become inconsequential in the affairs of mankind. Christians had become impotent; instituting little to change society. As the prophet Isaiah foretold, "darkness covered the earth and deep darkness the people" (Isaiah 60:2).

A dark cloud was smothering society, much like today. The people considered religion a duty and so it had no redeeming effect on their lives. Pomp and rituals took the place of mercy, grace, and wonder. Ministers had little or no faith. Most were godless skeptics that preached dead words just to collect stipends. Luther's reforms, which began in the Spirit, went the wrong direction among later Protestants. The spiritual revival that swept the land in the sixteenth and seventeenth centuries waned as generations emerged who loved their sins and ignored scripture.

One contemporary historian said, "The taste for the pornographic was avid; the appetite for the vulgar and the sensual was at a peak. Religion was dead." Bishop Berkely said that in England,

> "Morality and religion have collapsed to a degree that has never been known in any Christian country. Our prospect is very terrible and the symptoms grow worse from day to day. The youth born and brought up in these wicked times without any bias to good…when they grow ripe, will be monsters indeed. And it is so feared that the age of monsters is not far off."

Following European patterns, Colonial America had little moral restraint. The towns were overflowing with greed, lust, and self-gratification. Deism was a growing belief among the upper-crust of society. They believed that God created the world, but he left creation to its own devices. Most congregations were impotent and weak; doing little to change society. The Eighteenth Century world was ripe for a mighty move of God.

THE GREAT AWAKENING

Things appeared to be moving in the wrong direction, but God had a different plan. The Lord will not stand by while everything falls apart. He is a God of restoration and revival. In time, who He is will always come to the forefront.

The kingdom of darkness was ill-prepared for what would descend from heaven. The glory of the Lord Almighty would be poured out over a dry and dying Church. This earth-shaking revival would not only bring life back to the Church, but return it to its righteous passions.

What was about to unfold was a move that would convert the heathen and transform a complacent, compromised Church. It would confront the culture, shift the moral climate of society, and change the course of the Church.

This sovereign move of God would later be called the Great Awakening!

THE MARVEL OF THE AGE

We trace the first sparks of the American leg of the Great Awakening, to the preaching of Jonathan Edwards and Gilbert Tennent. The unwavering devotion and spiritual fervor of these men spread far and wide.

Another "flame of fire" in this move of God was an English preacher the press dubbed "The Marvel of the Age." His thundering oratory held thousands spell-bound on two continents. He preached 18,000 sermons to ten million hearers. This friend of John Wesley and converter of the masses was George Whitefield.

Desperate times call for bold preachers. In dark eras, society needs a flaming torch-bearer—one who can restore hope and trust in God. Society needed a man anointed of God with a voice who could rock the lethargy and sin. Biographer, J. C. Ryle wrote,

> "Of all the spiritual heroes of a hundred years ago, none saw so soon as Whitefield what the times demanded and none were so forward in the great works of spiritual aggression."

YOUNGER YEARS

George Whitefield was born December 27, 1714, in Gloucester, England. His parents ran an Inn and Tavern. He was continually around lying, thievery, gambling, and cursing. So, it is no surprise that Whitefield became worldly and entangled by sin at an early age.

Bell's Tavern, as it was called, was a gathering place for the malcontents and highwaymen—robbers and pimps who conducted vile acts around the tables. Whitefield made the customers roar in laughter when he derided and mimicked local preachers.

By the age of seventeen, he gained a passion for the stage, engrossing himself in novels and theatrical plays. Whitefield developed a thundering voice that held tavern audiences spellbound. He could have easily been an actor, but he was gripped by grace and mercy of Jesus Christ.

VOICE OF WONDERMENT

After his conversion, Whitefield's booming voice served him well in the ministry. As he opened his mouth, he stirred wonderment across England. David Garrick, a gifted Shakespearian actor of that day, recounted the following after hearing Whitefield preach: "I would give 100 guineas to be able to say the word 'Oh!' like George Whitefield."

In his travels in America, one woman made the following observation:

> "He is a born orator. You had already heard of his deep-toned, yet clear melodious voice. It is perfect music. It is wonderful to see what a spell he casts over the audience by proclaiming the simplest truths of the Bible. I have seen upwards of a thousand people hang on his words with breathless silence, broken only by an occasional half-suppressed sob."

Whitefield's voice was quite an asset in a time before microphones and sound systems. On a clear day, some said that his animated cries could be heard as far as five miles away!

Curious about this claim, the famous Benjamin Franklin tested this theory. Using the scientific method, he calculated that Whitefield could be heard as far as a mile away. He could easily address 30,000 people in open air meetings.

Describing his own methods of speech, Whitefield once said, "I love those that thunder out the word. The Christian World is in a dead sleep. Nothing but a loud voice can awaken them out of it."

Although Whitefield had an advantage with his voice, he also had to wrestle with setbacks. When he was young, he developed measles. The disease unfortunately left him cross eyed that caused a squint. When people stood before him, witnessing his "cross-eyed stare and the soul searching squint," they were uncomfortable. They thought it was either a sign of madness or an indicator of a supernatural presence. His followers liked to say his crossed eyes helped him "keep one eye on heaven and the other eye on hell."

Whatever one thought of Whitefield's defect, as soon as he opened his mouth the squint was forgotten and people were overcome with a power from a different world—the kingdom of God. When newspaper journalists witnessed what was transpiring, they called Whitefield, "The Marvel of the Age," "The Awakener," and "The Fire Bringer."

Whitefield's message was simple—repent and be saved. Although he understood theology, he did not consider it important. His goal was to inspire people to seek salvation and the forgiveness of sins. Like the Apostle Paul, Whitefield preached "Christ and Him crucified."

OXFORD UNIVERSITY

As a young man, Whitefield attended Oxford University in England. Not having money for tuition, he came to the institution as a "servitor." In lieu of paying, he had to attend to the needs of his classmates. He was their personal servant, bringing food, cleaning rooms, carrying books and other menial jobs.

Whitefield met a group of students at Oxford who called themselves the "Holy Club," and his life was changed forever. These young men were a group of "pious Methodists." They chose the name "Methodist" because they strove to "live according to the methods of the bible." This small group was led by two brothers, John and Charles Wesley. Unlike other students, the Methodists treated Whitefield kindly. Becoming friends, they led him into the "New Birth," and served alongside him in ministry for the rest of their lives.

As the years progressed, Whitefield and the Wesley brothers were used tremendously in revival. Although they had disputes about Calvinism and Arminianism, they did not let doctrinal differences get in the way of their message of salvation. A Professor, knowing the sharp theological differences between them, asked Whitefield if he thought he would see John Wesley in heaven, Whitefield replied, "I fear not for he will be so near the throne and we at such a distance that we shall hardly get a sight of him."

ORDINATION AND CONSECRATION

After years of study at Oxford, Whitefield was ordained an Anglican Minister. Meeting other ministers and speaking in churches, he came to the realization that the religion of his day did not address the inner needs of the people. In much of the Anglican Church, there was no teaching on having a personal relationship with Jesus. As he was searching for answers, Whitefield came upon Henry Scougal's work, "The Life of God and the Soul of Man." What he read shook him to his core. Afterward, he wrote the following in his Journal:

"God showed me that I must be born again or be damned! I learned a man may go to church, say his prayers, receive the sacraments, and yet not be a Christian. Shall I burn this book? Shall I throw it down? Or shall I search it? I did search it; and... addressed the God of heaven and earth."

Then Whitefield began to pray, "Lord, if I am not a Christian, or if I am not a real one, for Jesus Christ's sake show me what Christianity is that I may not be damned at last." This was a sincere prayer that defined the rest of his life.

Whitefield became desperate for intimacy with the living God. Casting the world and self aside, he ran toward his savior in a hungry search for complete conversion. He said,

"Oh! What joy!—joy unspeakable---joy full and big with glory was my soul filled when the weight of sin came off and an abiding sense of the pardoning love of God and a full assurance of faith broke in on my...soul! Surely it was...a day to be had in everlasting remembrance...My joys were like a spring tide, and overflowed the banks!"

In a sense, Whitefield's desire to become an actor had been answered. But it occurred in God's unique way. The stage was set, the players and their roles were established, and the audience was booked. Into the spotlight came a man carrying a torch of revival. sHe declared, "I have not come in my own name. No! I have come in the Name of the Lord of hosts and I must and will be heard!"

THE STIRRINGS OF REVIVAL

At the age of twenty-one, Whitefield gave his first sermon in the church of St. Mary de Crypt. The people were excited to hear him. When he spoke, the congregation was shaken to the core. A presiding Bishop, who was in attendance, said at least fifteen people were "driven mad!" The people were transfixed, and from that day on, Whitefield's popularity never waned. J.C. Ryle wrote, "No preacher has ever been so popular . . . in England, Scotland and America."

Together with the Wesley's, he preached throughout England, Scotland, and Wales. Thousands attended his services. Revival fires were breaking out wherever he preached. Because of the controversies that came with soul-stirring messages, the Church of England, refused to give Whitefield a pulpit—just like they had done to the Wesleys.

Never deterred, Whitefield began preaching in out-of-the way places—parks, fields, wagons, tables, balconies, hills, and boats. He would speak anywhere his body could be elevated so his voice could be heard. Everywhere he spoke, enormous crowds gathered. Over the months, the head count continued to grow. One occasion it was 1000, another 4000. Then as many as 10,000 gathered to hear this "flame of revival" preach. Wesley Duewel in his book, "Revival Fire" wrote,

> "Whitefield went to Hackney Marsh race course and preached to 10,000 who were there for the races. The people largely ignored the races and listened to the Gospel as Whitefield proclaimed it."

Whitefield later went to the race tracks to preach to the masses. In Marylebone Fields, he preached to 30,000. He gladly went to the Moorefields, one of the most despicable resorts in London, where 60,000 people stood enraptured in his sermon. The sound of spirited singing from the crowd, along with Whitefield's booming voice, could be heard across the countryside. It has already been said that people could hear him a mile away.

The common people loved him, but the religious system saw

him as a threat. When he exposed sin and the backslidden condition of the church, prominent clergymen were so incensed that they published pamphlets against him.

Whitefield's preaching was exceptionally simple. But with his dramatic voice, the scriptures came to life so that the listeners were drawn into the story. With his declarations, the verses became so real that it was like the audience was transported back to the dust of Galilee or sitting in the synagogue while Jesus was preaching.

J. C. Ryle declared the following about Whitefield's preaching: "He met men face-to-face, like one who had a message from God to them. 'I have come here to speak to you about your soul.'"

Winkie Pratney, in his outstanding book, Revival, says that Whitefield "dramatized so vividly that his sermons seemed to move and walk before your eyes, drawing such vivid pictures his hearers sometimes actually believed they saw and heard them."

As Whitefield preached, God's Spirit would come powerfully upon people, overwhelming them. Many standing were cut down in droves. One man said that Whitefield "preached like a lion. His sermons were life and fire; you must listen whether you like it or not. There was a holy violence about him which firmly took your attention by storm."

Friend or foe, no one could stand under the anointing that exuded from Whitefield. One convert said to him, "I came to hear you with a pocket full of stones to break your head but your sermon got the better of me, and God broke my heart."

OPPOSITION GROWS

The authorities and Anglican power brokers were intimated by his ministry. They felt that something had to be done to stop him. They drew the line in the sand and said they were not going to allow his efforts to go unchallenged.

Some New England pastors wrongly claimed that Whitefield

destroyed, "New England's orderly parish system, communities, and even families." A prominent newspaper editor in Charlestown, South Carolina labeled him, "Blasphemous, uncharitable, and unreasonable."

In many of the Colonial pulpits, Whitefield was accused of being, "an imposter, a devil, the beast, the man of sin, the Antichrist." In 1757, while preaching in Dublin, Ireland, a huge Roman Catholic mob rioted and attacked him. These out-of-control people wounded Whitefield severely and smashed his portable pulpit. Opponents threw anything they could get their hands on—rocks, feces, rotten food, and even dead cats.

On one occasion, Whitefield was almost killed by a man who beat him with a brass-headed cane. Another time he was assaulted by a woman wielding, "scissors and a pistol, and her teeth." Whitefield endured numerous public humiliations including the time an opponent climbed a tree and urinated on him.

Whitefield was unwavering in his commitment to preach. He stood strong whether people received his words or not. When the people became harsh, he said, that they were "being hardened as were Pharaoh and the Egyptians." Any opposition made him more adamant to set God's people free.

REVIVAL SPREADS

Revival, and bold biblical preaching were spreading throughout Scotland, Wales, and Ireland. Soon it would be felt more deeply across the Atlantic. With the fervor growing, Whitefield traveled to America. After he arrived, the colonists flocked to hear this purveyor of "divine things."

Many traveled twenty or thirty miles to hear Whitefield preach. From Massachusetts to Georgia, state by state, multitudes came to be in the revival services. Whitefield often preached morning, noon and evening. Some of his evening services attracted multitudes and continued until 2am. It wasn't unusual for him to speak four times on Sunday. This grueling schedule amounted to forty to sixty hours of speaking every week.

Some of the churches filled with more people than were living in the town. So, when the buildings could no longer handle the crowds, Whitefield began conducting "field preaching." Soon, adjacent fields were covered with thousands, some sat in coaches and others on horseback. A few of the spiritually hungry climbed the trees and sat along the edge of pastures. Most who heard Whitefield were overcome with tears. Multitudes cried out with exceeding joy, and were overcome with God's power.

The surging crowds that were attending Whitefield's meetings were overwhelming:

MIDDLETON CONNECTICUT—4000

NESHAMINY PA.—5,000

NEW BRUNSWICK, NEW JERSEY—7,000-8,000

PHILADELPHIA—20,000

Wherever he preached, multitudes fell to the ground. It was as if they were before a firing squad. These were scenes of uncontrollable distress, like soldiers in a field of battle. In these raucous outdoor meetings, there were people from all walks of life including governors and mayors. The rich and the poor were both on the ground, crying out for the salvation of their souls. Sometimes, all through the night, shouts of prayer and praise could be heard in the fields.

Spiritual hunger in the English colonies was on the verge of hysteria. Shackles were being shaken loose. Pre-revolutionary

America was waking out of a stupor. God was calling and the people were saying, "Here we are!"

BENJAMIN FRANKLIN AND THE AMERICAN COLONIES

Over the next few years, Whitefield visited America several times. While ministering in Philadelphia, Whitefield met Benjamin Franklin and the two remained friends the rest of their lives.

Franklin, at first had many doubts about this revivalist, but he changed his mind. Noticing what was happening to the people, he wrote,

> "wonderful . . . change soon was made in the manners of our inhabitants. From being thoughtless or indifferent about religion, it seemed as if all the world were growing religious, so that one could not walk thro' the town in an evening without hearing psalms sung in different families of every street."

On his last trip to America, Whitefield's passion for his Savior was contagious and spread like wildfire. He said, "O what a new scene of usefulness is opening up in various parts of the New World! All fresh work...the divine influence is as at the first!"

Whitefield preached for three weeks in Philadelphia and then continued to New York. Although he traveled hundreds of miles daily, he still held staggering Holy Ghost infused meetings. He never lost his zeal for speaking of Christ, saying, "God forbid that I should travel with anybody a quarter of an hour without speaking of Christ to them."

The Apostle Paul said, "I will most gladly spend and be spent for souls" (2 Corinthians 12:15). He was willing to give all for the gospel. This was the same attitude that George Whitefield possessed.

WHITEFIELD'S LAST SERMON

When Whitefield traveled to Newburyport, Massachusetts on September 29, 1770, he did not know that this was going to be his last day of ministry. Exhausted, he stood in a field, "atop a large barrel," and faced a vast multitude of souls. He proceeded to contend for their souls for over two hours. Even though Whitefield was wearied and in poor health, he said, "I would rather wear out than rust out."

Later that evening, while Whitefield was dining, a massive crowd of people gathered outside, wanting to hear him preach. Looking out, he wearily said, "I am tired and must go to bed." He picked up a lit candle and climbed the stairs to his bed. But as he glanced back at the crowd, the evangelist in him rose up and he addressed the crowd.

Whitefield poured out his heart to the tear-soaked crowd until the candle burned out. Saying goodnight, he went to bed. A violent asthma attack woke him. Whitefield prayed, but the attack grew worse. By 5 o'clock, he was struggling for breath. At 6 o'clock, that radiant, melodious, and booming voice was singing praises with the saints around the throne. He was glorifying Jesus, the one who he had introduced to thousands. George Whitefield had set himself on fire for Jesus and pressed on until he burned himself out for God.

At his memorial service, hymns could not be heard over the travail of six thousand mourners. Throughout the American colonies, England, Scotland, and Wales church bells tolled. Ships in the harbors, around the world, fired their guns in salute. John Wesley gave a tribute of Whitefield to thousands and in city after city memorial services were held in front of thousands. Whitefield himself once said, "Sudden death is sudden glory!"

George Whitefield was one of those 'fire brands" that God blesses His Church with in times of need. He was a world changer, history maker, soldier of the cross, and an elite man of fire who convicted the Church for the purpose it was called.

In his biography of this great servant of God, Luke Tyerman described Whitefield as follows:

> "Half a dozen men like Whitefield would at any time move a nation, stir its churches, and reform its morals. Whitefield's power was not in his talents, nor even his oratory, but in his piety...such men are the gift of God, and are infinitely more valuable than all the gold in the church coffers."

George Whitefield was one of the greatest revivalists who stood on American soil. Over two centuries since his death, he is still influencing what we understand about awakenings.

> "See, I have this day set you over the nations and over the kingdoms, to root out and to pull down...to build and to plant." (Jeremiah 1:10)

3

HUDSON TAYLOR (PART ONE)

Hudson Taylor

"The great commission is not an option to be considered; it is a command to be obeyed." —Hudson Taylor

"The will of God—nothing less, nothing more, nothing else."—
F.E. Marsh

"If God calls you to be a missionary, don't stoop to be a king."—
Charles Spurgeon

"Our Savior has given us a commandment to preach the gospel
even to the ends of the earth. He will provide the fulfillment of
His own purpose. Let us only obey."—Allen Gardiner

"Never pity missionaries; envy them. They are where the action
is—where life and death, sin and grace, heaven and hell
converge."—Robert C. Shannon

"My son set out as a missionary of Christ; but alas! He has
dwindled down to a mere British ambassador."—William Carey

"If I had 1000 lives, I'd give them all for China."—Hudson
Taylor

"Why did you not come sooner?" This piercing question
came from a middle-aged Chinese man who had just
heard the gospel for the first time. The fact that an Englishman
would come from such a faraway land struck this listener. Why
would he learn to speak an unfamiliar language and put on
clothing of a distant culture? This missionary clearly carried an
unquenchable zeal.

The message utterly upended this Chinese recipient, but the
interchange also rattled the missionary. He clutched his abdomen
as he listened to this heartfelt response. In fact, this Asian man's
words stabbed like a hot poker. This Englishman already sensed
that what he was doing was vital, but now the mission became

significant in eternity. Millions of Chinese families had never heard the gospel and their futures lay in the balance. The reality of the overwhelming need for salvation tore his soul asunder.

Hudson Taylor, this pioneering missionary, was rent with grief as this broken man stood before him. He felt guilt about the failure of the Christian Church to share the gospel. It sickened him to realize that believers had lost sight of the "Great Commission."

This man, who had just heard the name of Jesus for the first time, was a key leader in a Buddhist sect. For years, this man sought truth, studying Confucianism, Buddhism, and Taoism. It was not until he received the gospel of Jesus that he found meaning and rest.

As this Buddhist official committed his life to Jesus, he asked Taylor, "Why did you not come sooner?" He also wanted to know how long they had known the gospel in England. When Taylor told him that they had known the message of Jesus for centuries, all the color left the face of this new convert. He said,

> "What? For all these centuries your people have had these glad tidings and only now have come to preach it to us? My father sought truth for more than twenty years and died without finding it. Oh, why did you not come sooner?"

This is the kind of question that Charles Haddon Spurgeon, the brilliant orator, once wrestled with, "Will the heathen who have never heard the Gospel be saved? It is more the question with me whether we—who have the Gospel and fail to give it to those who have not—can be saved?"

After hearing the impassioned words of this new convert and watching him eagerly testify to Buddhists about the peace he found, Hudson Taylor was determined that every province in China would hear the gospel.

Carrying the message of Jesus throughout Asia seemed like

an impossible task. The population was immense, and the government opposed the work. But Taylor believed that the impossible was already made possible in God. After all, he had already been miraculously launched out into the mission field. Many questioned whether fruit would come from his efforts. But Taylor identified with the words of the Prophet Isaiah when God commissioned him: "Then I heard the voice of the Lord saying, 'Whom shall I send? And who will go for us?' And I said, 'Here am I. Send me!'" (Isaiah 6:8).

Since the Lord commanded, "Go ye into all the world," the responsibility to accomplish this mission was not on the shoulders of man. It was up to heaven to fulfill this mandate. Although Taylor didn't know how this would be accomplished, he knew that "Yahweh Yireh" would take care of everything. God had already provided for this crusade for souls. All he had to do was step out in faith. Reflecting on this, Taylor wrote,

"I am no longer anxious about anything, as I realize that He is able to carry out His will for me. It does not matter where he places me or how. That is for Him to consider, not me, for in the easiest positions He will give me grace, and in the most difficult ones His grace is sufficient."

Chloe Joy, a gifted Taylor biographer, wrote about the legacy of this fire-baptized Ambassador for Christ.

"James Hudson Taylor, founder of the China Inland Mission, was a man passionately driven to seeking God's will on earth. He is best known for the drastic difference he made in evangelizing China and founding the China Inland Mission. Hudson converted thousands of Chinese, and even today the mission organization continues to follow his example."

HAD I ONE THOUSAND LIVES

Over a lifetime of service to Christ, Hudson Taylor left an incredible legacy. From the age of five, he had dedicated his life to reaching the people of China. He was distressed, knowing that thousands in China were dying every day without ever hearing the name of Jesus. Taylor told friends, "Had I a thousand lives, I should give them all for China." They would scold him, saying that he was embarking on an impossible dream. When he heard this, he responded: "Dream a dream so big that unless God intervenes, it will fail."

What a task lay before Taylor. When he first set foot in China, there were less than one hundred missionaries available to witness to over four hundred million people. To make matters worse, a handful of denominational officials controlled the missionary efforts. The so-called ministry efforts—mostly educational—were only in heavily populated coastal areas.

Inland China, the huge geographical center of the nation, was untouched by the missionaries. In fact, there were no plans to evangelize this part of the nation. Many thought that it would be useless to go there, but Taylor had a different outlook. Although others were resistant to go, Taylor saw a wide-open door. He wrote, "There awaits a great harvest, but few here are ready to reap." Taylor anticipated the hardships that lay ahead, but he also knew the resourcefulness of his God, declaring, "There are three stages in the work of God: impossible, difficult, done!"

The negativity of the others did not faze Taylor. He didn't get sidetracked by naysayers, pointing out the hardships and difficulties that awaited him in the country's interior. He knew that his mission depended on the goodness and grace of God. Taylor wrote,

"Depend on it. God's work done in God's way will never lack God's supply. He is too wise a God to frustrate His purposes for lack of funds, and He can just as easily supply them ahead of time as afterwards, and He much prefers doing so."

Taylor was a great man of faith. He believed God wanted to accomplish the impossible. But he had not always been so confident in the Lord. He was like misshaped clay that had to be molded and strengthened in the fire.

EARLY YEARS

James Hudson Taylor was born in Barnsley, Yorkshire, England on May 21, 1832. He was the oldest of four children. Before he was born, his devout parents dedicated him to the Lord, believing that he would be a missionary to China. Even as a child he would declare, "When I am a man, I mean to be a missionary and go to China." All were convinced that Taylor had a remarkable destiny.

His father, James Taylor, a Methodist minister and chemist, was from a long lineage of fervent Christians. His mother, Amelia Hudson Taylor, was also devout. All the children in the Taylor household were brought up in, "The way they should go" (Proverbs 22:6).

Hudson, as a child, was frail, and often ill. This kept him from attending school until he was eleven years of age. All of his younger brothers died while they were young. He formed a close bond with his sister, Amelia—named after their mother. Their closeness would continue for the rest of their lives, despite the fact that Taylor turned away from the Lord for a few years.

At the age of seventeen, Taylor began traveling the path of darkness. While attending school, the outside influences of unbelievers and a desire for independence, chipped away at his Christian foundation. Breaking from his childhood patterns, he associated with the ungodly and no longer took time to pray to God.

With Taylor's poor health, his family took him out of school and he started working with his father in a chemistry laboratory. Later he was employed in a bank. Enticed by the surrounding worldliness, so-called friends introduced many dark influences. They loved to mock the "controlling ways and silliness" of Christianity. With the constant barrage of temptations and pleasures, sin overcame him. He jumped into the cesspool of the world with both feet. Taylor said,

"I had many opportunities in early years of learning the value of prayer and of the word of God; for it was the delight of my dear parents to point out that if there were any such being as God, to trust Him, to obey Him and to be fully given up to His service, must, out of necessity be the best and wisest course both for myself and others. But in spite of these helpful examples and precepts, my heart was unchanged. Often I had tried to make myself a Christian, and failing, of course in such efforts, I began at last to think that for some reason or other I could not be saved, and that the best I could do was to take my fill of this world, as there was no hope for me beyond the grave."

Naturally, his beloved sister, Amelia, was concerned. She prayed diligently for him three times every day. But her intercession seemed to be to no avail. Taylor dropped deeper and deeper into the ways of the world. He no longer walked in the faith of his family.

CONVERSION

Taylor's mother was burdened for the salvation of her son as well. One day, while away on a trip, she felt an intense burden to pray for him. She knew God's word, and His word was in her. She understood the power in 1 John 5:14-15: "Now this is the confidence that we have in Him that if we ask anything according to His will. He hears us. And if He hears us, whatever we ask, we know that we have the petitions that we have asked of Him."

Taylor's mother went into a room, locked the door, and prayed. She didn't beg for his salvation; she declared it. At that moment, she knew that no matter how long it took, her son was saved. Praising and thanking God for His faithfulness, she continued her travels with the conviction that her prayers had already been answered.

Meanwhile, about eighty miles away, Hudson was in his father's library looking for an entertaining book to peruse. Not finding anything to his liking, he turned to the desk and noticed a basket filled with pamphlets and small books. He pulled out a gospel tract that looked interesting to him. He thought, "There will be an interesting story at the beginning and then a sermon or moral at the close. I will read the story and leave the sermon or moral for those who like it." He expected nothing to transpire, but soon his entire world would change. Taylor wrote,

> "In an utterly unconcerned state of mind, believing indeed at the time that if there were any salvation, it was not for me, and with a distinct intention to put away the tract as soon as it should seem prosy... while reading it I was struck with the phrase, "The finished work of Christ"... Then came the further thought, "if the whole work was finished and the whole debt paid, what is there left for me to do?"

Taylor had been so preoccupied, in the past, with trying to do good and maintain morality by his own strength. He found that this was impossible to accomplish. But after reading the phrase, "The finished work of Christ," Taylor suddenly realized that Jesus paid it all. Light had finally come. Taylor jumped up from his chair and praised his King! He would later write,

"And with this dawned the joyful conviction, as light was flashed into my soul by the Holy Spirit, that there was nothing in the world to be done but to fall down on one's knees and accept this Savior and His salvation, praise Him forever more."

Fourteen days later, his mother returned home, and he couldn't wait to tell her the exciting news. When he blurted it out, she replied, "I know my boy, I have been rejoicing for the past fourteen days in the glad tidings you have to tell." Taylor later wrote, "My dear mother assured me that it was not from any human source she had learned the tidings … You will agree with me that it would be strange indeed if I were not a believer in the power of prayer."

After his salvation experience, Taylor longed to be in God's presence. He experienced times of intense desperation as well as indescribable joy. With an insatiable hunger to grow in the things of God, he spent hours interceding and reading the Bible. It changed his whole life. Taylor wrote,

"Let us giving our work, our thoughts, our places, ourselves, our lives, our loved ones, our influence, our all, right into His hand, and then, when we have given all over to Him, there will be nothing left for us to trouble about or to make trouble about."

POWER IN PRAYER

As he grew in faith, Taylor learned what his parents already knew —there is incredible power in prayer. Coming out of a time of intercession, Taylor once said, "There are three great truths. First, there is a God. Second, He has spoken to us. Third, he means what he says." This kind of insight remained with him the rest of his life. Taylor once wrote,

"The prayer power has never been tried to its full capacity... if we want to see mighty wonders of Divine power and grace wrought in the place of weakness, failure, and disappointment, let us answer God's standing challenge, "Call to Me and I will answer you, and show you great and inaccessible things, which you do not know."

One afternoon, Taylor entered into a time of prayer. An intense fervor filled his heart as he went up to his room to be alone with God. He longed to have an audience with the Lord Almighty. Taylor later wrote,

"Well do I remember that occasion, how in the gladness of my heart I poured out my soul before God, and again and again confessing my grateful love to Him who had done everything for me--- who saved me when I had given up all hope and even desire for salvation---I besought Him to give me some work to do for Him... no matter what it might be... however trivial... Well do I remember... the deep solemnity that came over my soul... The presence of God became unutterably real and blessed... a deep consciousness that I was not my own took possession of me, which has never since been effaced... never shall I forget the feeling that came over me then. Words can never describe it... something seemed to say, 'Your prayer is answered.'"

As Taylor worshipped, he longed to give everything back to the God who had given everything for him. The calling that had been spoken over his life as a child, had been rekindled.

Taylor sensed that it was time for the cloud of darkness to be dispelled. For centuries, Satan claimed territories, but the light of the kingdom of God was now breaking through the dark haze. Through Christ, light shone so "He might make known the riches of His glory on the vessels of mercy, which He had prepared beforehand" (Romans 9:23).

Hudson Taylor was called for a time such as this. While on his knees, crying out to the God of salvation, his body shook. A thunderous voice that felt like an earthquake reverberated in his spirit, Taylor heard the unmistakable voice of God saying, "Go for me to China!"

"And other sheep I have which are not of this fold; them also I must bring, and they will hear My voice; and there will be one flock *and* one shepherd" (John 10:16).

4

HUDSON TAYLOR (PART TWO)

Hudson Taylor

"Some may now say that my prayer was finally answered, but that would be incorrect. I received the answer to my prayer the day I prayed it." —James O. Fraser

"It has always been my ambition to preach the gospel where Christ was not known." —Paul of Tarsus (Romans 15:20)

"This morning about nine, I withdrew to the woods for prayer. I was in such anguish that when I arose from my knees, I felt extremely weak and overcome... I cared not how or where I lived, or what hardships I went through so that I could but gain souls for Christ." —David Brainerd

"God send me anywhere, only go with me. Lay any burden on me, only sustain me. And sever any tie in my heart except the tie that binds my heart to you."—David Livingstone

"Does it not stir up our hearts to go forth and help them, does it not make us long to leave our luxury, our exceeding abundant light, and go to them that sit in darkness." —Amy Carmichael

Three years passed after Hudson Taylor first heard the voice of God say, "Go, for me, to China!" Although he was already aching to launch out to the mission field, this wasn't yet possible. God led Taylor to walk through a challenging season of self-denial and stamina-building.

During this time, Taylor read about the exploits of many missionaries in China, including the exploits of Robert Morrison, who preached in China nearly a half century before. Just like Morrison, Taylor was also being burdened with naysayers who tried to dissuade him from the missionary career. Like Morrison, he silenced their remarks by laying everything on God's shoulders. Taylor enjoyed a story from the life of Morrison that encouraged him:

"The man... looking at him with a sneering smile that only half concealed his contempt, inquired, 'Now Mr. Morrison, do you really expect you will make an impression on the idolatry of the Chinese Empire? 'No sir,' said Morrison, 'but I expect God will.'"

DOCTOR TAYLOR

Envisioning his future work on the mission field, Hudson thought that he might be able to help the diseased in China with greater medical expertise. So, he took up studying medicine at the Royal London Hospital in Whitechapel.

While learning from the physicians, Taylor pricked his finger sewing sheets of paper together for a lecture notebook. The next day, in class, he helped students dissect the body of a man. But while exhuming the corpse, Taylor felt weak. Suddenly, he remembered the open wound on his finger. Nauseous, he felt poison from the cadaver enter into his blood steam. The surgeon, overseeing the lab, became alarmed and solemnly said, "Go home and arrange your affairs as quickly as possible, for you are a dead man." Hudson answered, "I do not think I will die, for unless I am much mistaken I have work to do in China; and if so, however severe the struggle, I must be brought through." The doctor, who was a non-believer, replied, "That is all well but you have no time to lose, for you will soon be incapable of winding up your affairs."

Hudson went home and washed his hand in hot water. Then, while evangelizing a neighbor, he felt deathly ill. Hudson began to fervently intercede, reminding God of the calling on his life. He said that myriads of souls in China were in the balance if he should die. Shortly after his prayers, the disease lifted. Although still somewhat weak, Taylor went back to class and shared the outcome of his prayers with the doctor that gave him a death sentence. He explained the goodness and faithfulness of God.

The surgeon, with tears in his eyes, said, "I would give all the world for a faith like yours."

During this time, Taylor also studied the Chinese language with the assistance of a furloughed missionary. His instructor said that anyone wanting to preach in Chinese needed "bodies of iron, lungs of brass, heads of oak, hands of spring steel, eyes of eagles, hearts of apostles, memories of angels, and lives of Methuselah." Since Hudson had always been sickly, it was a high mountain to climb, but he went at it courageously. He said, "God is not looking for men of great faith, He is looking for common men to trust in His faithfulness."

Although raised a Methodist, he later affiliated with the Westbourne Grove Baptist Church. Taylor also formed ties with the Open Brethren, a Low Church evangelical movement. His theology and ministerial practice remained non-sectarian.

PREPARING FOR MISSIONARY LIFE

Also, to be ready for the rigors of the mission field, Taylor relinquished all luxuries and comforts, including his beloved feather bed. He moved to a rundown neighborhood in the city of Hull. This community had two rows of dilapidated cottages facing each other. People mockingly called it "Drainside" because a ditch with garbage ran across it. The foul stench kept most outsiders away.

While living in Drainside, Taylor subsisted on oatmeal, rice, and brown bread. This missionary-in-training neglected many of the basic amenities. Any money he received, he gave to the most unfortunate. He used every conversation and chance to serve his neighbors as an opportunity to share the gospel.

Throughout this time, Taylor sought God continually, spending hours a day in prayer. He learned the power of intercession from his mother and became known as a "man of prayer." Taylor gave up all his provisions and relied on God for his sustenance. Some called Taylor a "Man of faith," but he said that he was, "only a servant of a faithful God." He had no doubt that whatever he prayed would come into this hands.

In intercession, he spoke the Word of God back to the Lord, reminding Him that He is a faithful covenant-keeper. Nevertheless, when he declared something in prayer, he didn't want to be presumptuous. He was wary of his own desires, doing nothing without the approval of the Father.

> "Yes, the Almighty will be your gold and your precious silver; for then you will have your delight in the Almighty and lift up your face to God. You will make your prayer to Him, He will hear you, and you will pay your vows. You will declare a thing, and it will be established for you; so light will shine on your ways." (Job 22:25-28)

THE VOYAGE TO CHINA

After three years, the London Missionary Society agreed that it was time to send the young intercessor out into the field. After this extended time of preparation, Taylor was excited to finally fulfill God's plan for his life. He booked passage on the cargo ship "Dumfries," for September 19, 1853. Taylor then set out on a five month voyage from Liverpool to Shanghai.

Although Taylor was well liked by the captain, some of the crewmen were hostile to him. Taylor was unmoved by their criticism. He tried to help anywhere that he could. He cleaned the deck, reefed sails, and assisted with the navigation. Some of those who were against him began to see him in a different light.

On Sundays, Taylor organized morning and evening services on the ship. Although many did not accept his preaching, he was never unwilling to share about his faith in Christ—even if the audience was ambivalent. One Sunday, when his passion got the better of him, he extended a service by forty minutes. No one turned up for the next meeting. Later in the voyage there would be a change of mind about this man of God.

Eighty-two days into the voyage, a violent storm erupted on the seas. With towering waves, gale force winds, and a pitch black sky, disaster was imminent. Every man on the ship was making their peace with God. Taylor wrote the following in his diary:

> "The wind whistles shrilly through the rigging, the sails roar again with the violence of the wind and rain, the masts crack, the ship reels and lies over, and the seas as they strike her make every timber vibrate."

The hurricane-force winds were tossing the ship back and forth. Taylor struggled to make his way to the deck. Barely holding on the rails, he witnessed an unforgettable display. The chaotic sea was wild and foaming. Waves towered thirty feet above the ship, almost swamping it. Amid these other problems, the wind was pushing the vessel toward the rocky coast. Captain Morris shouted to the crew, "I've never seen a wilder sea. Unless God helps us, there's no hope. We can't live but a half hour."

Taylor raced to his cabin, fell on his knees, and stormed the throne of mercy. He proclaimed,

> "God my Father, I commend my soul to You and my friends to Your care … Lord, have mercy on us and spare us, for the sake of the unconverted crew members as well as Your own glory as the God who hears and answers prayer. Your word says that if anyone calls upon You in the day of trouble, You will deliver them and they shall glorify You. You are a covenant God who stands by His word, so I ask You now to fulfill the promise of that word in our behalf. That You may receive the glory."

Amid violent seas, something wonderful unfolded. Within the

darkest night, a bright golden moon appeared. Although the winds were still raging, and they were still careening toward the rocks, hope arose. In the bleakest darkness, light will shine.

With less than a few hundred feet from menacing rocks, the winds miraculously shifted and the ship could return to safer waters. God had intervened and saved the ship. At the next Sunday service, every individual on the ship joyfully attended and proclaimed the glory of God.

BEGINNING HIS WORK IN CHINA

The ship finally arrived in China after a long voyage. As soon as he stepped on the soil, Taylor was overwhelmed. He wrote, "My feelings on stepping ashore I cannot describe. My heart felt as though it had not room and must burst its bonds, while tears of gratitude and thankfulness fell from my eyes."

Taylor had entered a whole new world that was radically different from anything he had ever experienced. No one really knew him. He carried letters of introduction with him but the recipients were either dead or had left the continent.

Fortunately, Taylor was able to make his way to the London Mission Compound. While there, the missionaries he talked to were despondent and unsatisfied. They had not prepared for the hardships of the mission field and felt like the assignment was too difficult.

Most of these missionaries kept to the plush, stylish coastal towns, leaving the interior of the country untouched. Hudson didn't understand their mindset. Hudson would have none of that. He always went for the unsaved and went for the worst.

Taylor didn't want to be around people who had lost their faith in the mission of God. He believed that it was a precious gift to do the will of God. He said, "The real secret of an unsatisfied life lies too often in an unsurrendered will."

He left the compound and acquired a dilapidated shack.

When the neighbors discovered he was a doctor, they sought his assistance. He was able to minister to their bodies and their souls.

Taylor touched lives throughout the entire neighborhood and many were open to him. In time, he started a school for the needy children. In this facility, he had a captive audience to many who had only heard of idols and ancient superstitions.

EMBRACING CHINESE CULTURE

Taylor was pouring his heart into this effort, but it wasn't seeing many results. Many of the listeners were inattentive. He couldn't figure out what was wrong.

One day a man asked Taylor to explain why he had buttons on the back of his coat. He realized that his English clothing distracted listeners. Discarding the biases of other missionaries, Taylor dressed like a Chinese teacher. He shaved his head, leaving enough hair to tie at the back in a braid. Taylor wore baggy trousers, white calico socks, satin shoes, and a loose gown with wide sleeves. Embracing some of these cultural trimmings won the hearts of the people. The mindset of his neighbors wasn't to become European Christians but Chinese Christians. The people saw that the marvelous truths of Jesus were not a foreign message after all.

Taylor labored with joy and happiness despite disappointments and threats on his life. He longed to see the Chinese people saved. Frequently he journeyed by boat into the interior of the country, preaching in villages where the name of Jesus had never been heard. One night, deep in the interior, they invited him to eat a meal. He accepted, and saw that the meal consisted of cold rice cakes and snakes fried in lamp oil. It wasn't appetizing, but he ate what he could, fearing someone would recognize him as a foreigner if he refused.

THE TAIPING REBELLION

The China that Taylor encountered when he stepped off the boat was more beautiful and dangerous than he ever expected. At this time a civil war was underway called the Taiping Rebellion. Reflecting on this, Taylor recorded the following in his diary: "The report of cannon shakes the house . . . the windows ring violently. I found . . . the half-buried headless corpse of a man."

One day as he watched a fire from a balcony, a cannon ball hit a wall near him, showering him with debris. Hudson's mother kept the metal ball for decades as a token of God's protection of her son. On another occasion, his home was burned to the ground. But none of this bothered Taylor.

Through every crisis, Taylor kept preaching and distributing gospel literature. Amid the chaos, the message of salvation spread. Hudson didn't want to share a humanistic, watered-down message. He wanted people to give themselves to the Lamb who deserves the reward of his suffering.

Taylor was fruitful in all he sought to accomplish. He rose above the contention and make a stand for Christ.

A FRUITFUL MAN

Quite the innovator, Taylor was the first leader to institute "faith missions," which is the sending of missionaries with no promise of financial support. Instead, these men and women would rely on prayer to move on the hearts of givers. Taylor founded the China Inland Mission (now called the Overseas Missionary Fellowship) in 1865. With millions needing to hear the message of Christ, he named the organization's magazine "China's Millions." This publication is still published today, but its title is now "East Asia's Millions."

In the midst of his ceaseless mission work he was also a devoted husband and father. In 1858, he met and fell in love with

Maria Dyer, a fellow missionary. They married and had 13 children. After Maria died of cholera, Taylor married Jane Elizabeth Faulding in 1872.

In 1905, while visiting Yangzhou and Zhenjiang, Taylor died reading scripture aloud in a seeker's home. Few were as devoted to the salvation of East Asia as this compassionate intercessor was. Many mourned his passing.

Though dead, Taylor's gospel mission continued through his descendants. In particular, he was honored by James Hudson Taylor III (1929-2009) serving in Hong Kong and James Hudson Taylor IV in other parts of Asia. Extended members of the Taylor family still serve in the eastern hemisphere.

When Taylor was buried, they placed him next to his first wife, Maria, in Zhenjiang, in a small English cemetery near the Yangtze River. Large industrial buildings were built over the small cemetery in the 1960s and the grave markers were destroyed. However, Taylor's was stored away in a museum. His great-grandson, James Hudson Taylor III, found it and asked a local Chinese church to re-erect the marker in their building in 1999. The land for the cemetery was re-developed a few years later and the demolition of the old buildings revealed that Maria's and Hudson's tombs were still intact. On August 28, 2013, the graves were excavated, along with the surrounding soil, and moved to a local church where they were re-buried in a memorial garden.

The importance of Taylor continues to be recognized and China's surging Christian population wants to celebrate the life of this great man. Today, many East Asian tourists have traveled to the United States, visiting his home town of Barnsley. They want to see where this man of God grew up.

James Hudson Taylor is widely recognized as one of the most momentous Europeans to visit China in the nineteenth century. To fully write about his legacy would require considerable time, paper, and ink. It would take volumes of books just to scratch the surface. What God did through this willing vessel is amazing.

Historian, Kenneth Scott Latourette, wrote that Hudson Taylor was "one of the greatest missionaries of all time, and . . . one of the four or five most influential foreigners who came to China in the nineteenth century." He's not alone with this sentiment.

Missiologist, Ralph D. Winter argued, "More than any other human being, James Hudson Taylor... made the greatest contribution to the cause of world mission in the 19th century."

Arthur F. Glasser of Fuller Theological Seminary said that Taylor "was ambitious without being proud...he was biblical without being bigoted... He was a follower of Jesus, without being superficial... He was charismatic without being selfish."

Ruth Tucker of Northern Illinois University claims, "No other missionary in the nineteen centuries since the Apostle Paul has had a wider vision and has carried out a more systematized plan of evangelizing a broad geographical area than Hudson Taylor."

So many other things could be said, but James Hudson Taylor was a man who knew how "to move man, through God, by prayer alone."

"Go therefore and make disciples of all the nations, baptizing them in the name of the Father and the Son and of the Holy Spirit." —Matthew 28:19

5

CANE RIDGE CAMPMEETING

Frontier Camp Meeting

"The only reason we don't have revival is because we are willing to live without it." —Leonard Ravenhill

"Revival awakens in our hearts an increased awareness of the presence of God, a new love for God, a new hatred for sin, and a hunger for His word."-Del Fehsenfield Jr.

"During true revival, thousands of lost people are suddenly swept into the kingdom of God. Scenes of the lost coming to the Savior in great and unprecedented numbers are common." — Henry Blackaby

"The average man is not going to be impressed by our publicity, our posters, or our programs, but let there be a demonstration of the supernatural in the realm of religion, and at once man is arrested." Duncan Campbell

"If Jesus came back today, He wouldn't cleanse the temple, He would cleanse the pulpit."—Leonard Ravenhill

"Holy Ghost fire is what the world needs now! Holy Ghost fire—an unction from God; the endowment of power; the fire that purifies the heart, empowers the Church, and attracts the lost."-Frank Di Pietro

∽

On August 6, 1801, the air was hot, humid, and dry in central Kentucky. Though heavy rain was inching in, you wouldn't know it from the thick dust that permeated the air.

For days, the sounds of creaking wagons were heard as families made their way to a communion service at the Presbyterian church in a log meetinghouse. This gathering would turn into the most monumental camp meeting in the history of America.

For over a year, there had been news of extraordinary supernatural happenings at communion gatherings at the Red River, Gasper River, and Muddy River congregations. Many individuals had been powerfully touched. So the anticipation for the next meeting in this part of the frontier was high.

One traveler wrote to a friend that he was on his way "to the greatest meeting of its kind ever known. Religion has got to such a height here that people attend from a great distance; on this occasion I doubt not, but there will be 10,000 people."

This farmer's calculation was off. He underestimated the crowds by as many as 20,000. But from August 6-12, 1801, around thirty-thousand from Central Kentucky, Southern Ohio, and Northern Tennessee gathered on the grounds of the Cane Ridge Presbyterian Church, twenty miles east of Lexington. No one wanted to miss what was transpiring. The godly and the curious were coming together in one of the largest gatherings of this era.

What became known as the Cane Ridge Revival was a legendary event in American revival history. Never, in the frontier, had thousands gathered for a communion service. Never had masses of people camped outdoors on church grounds. It was strange that so many were affected by the Holy Spirit with physical manifestations such as, sobbing, wailing, travailing, shouting, shaking, jerking, falling to the floor in trances powerless and motionless, and many, for days at a time without food or drink or life signs only to rise from the ground declaring the wonders of salvation and the mercy of their God.

Historian, Paul K. Conkin, in his book, Cane Ridge, America's Pentecost, wrote, "Cane Ridge is arguably… the most important religious gathering in all American History." For decades, whenever camp meetings or local revivals were erupting, the rallying prayer would be, "Lord, make it like Cane Ridge!"

EGYPTIAN DARKNESS

In the decades after the American Revolution, cities along the Eastern seaboard were flourishing. Expansion gripped the imagination of the nation as thousands of families moved west. But as freedom was on their lips, many were tragically turning away from God.

The fervor of the First Great Awakening had waned. Fiery sermons that had come from revivalists like Jonathan Edwards, Gilbert Tennent, and George Whitefield were no longer in vogue. In this season, most of the churches were gripped by denominational division, animosity, and confusion. Church membership was at an all-time low. The love of many grew cold as religious indifference spread like a plague.

Alcoholism, profanity, murder, thievery, and sexual immorality were rampant. Tragically, immorality and licentiousness deepened in the youth. Teenagers and young adults embraced the wretchedness of the world. Along the edge of the wilderness, drunkenness, infidelity, and thievery were common.

Many ministers blamed the spiritual and moral turmoil on the disruptions from the revolutionary war and the growing religious rationalism. They rightly claimed that doctrines of demons were undermining the faith. It was true that some embraced *Deism*, the belief that God created the cosmos but left everything to its own devices. Others embraced *Universalism*, a doctrine that claims all will be saved, regardless of faith. Of course, *Atheism*, disbelief in the existence of God, also gained traction.

The ministers were shirking their responsibilities. They were supposed to be the bearers of life but were often as lifeless as their backslidden congregants. Consider the following excerpts from pastoral letters:

"I have this winter past, preached with difficulty, but heart being but little engaged in the endeavor. I know that I am not where I ought to be but cannot affect my sad case."

"The dead state of religion is truly discouraging here, as well as elsewhere. When I look into my wretched heart and consider how much I have dishonored God, by my dead and careless life, I have reason to cover my head in the dust."

"I can tell you but little about my poor congregation. I see but little prospect of encouragement. I dare not say none. They are a people who are vain, dark, and wild; full of unbelief and sin, dead and careless, spotted all over; more like devils than Christians."

Men who were supposed to be vessels of righteousness offered very little to the people in their care. The fervent intercession and devotion of the past had faded. There was little memory of the stirring revivals that occurred a half a century before.

While the spiritual condition of people was dreadful in the cities, it was even worse in the wilderness. Outside of established communities, churches were few and far between. When one could find a congregation, the devotion would be sorely lacking.

Recognizing the crisis, the Presbyterian General Assembly set aside a day for fasting and prayer for salvation of the frontier—a place they likened to "Egyptian darkness." Tired preachers declared what should have been the cry of every generation. "Will you not revive us again, that your people may rejoice in you? (Psalm 85:6).

As the Nineteenth Century dawned, the United States was truly at a crossroads. Would we live for God or be entrapped in our sins? Everything was hanging in the balance.

Trouble was abreast in the frontier, but nothing came as a surprise to Almighty God. Whether acknowledged by man or not, He reigns over the affairs of nations. The Lord moves among men like He did in ages past. In Elijah's time, the Lord said, "I have reserved seven thousand in Israel, all whose knees have not bowed to Baal" (1 Kings 19:18).

The bleakest night engulfed them, but a light would soon shine in the darkness. Things would be similar to what the Gospel of Matthew recorded, "The people who sat in darkness saw a great light, and upon those who sat in the region and shadow of death, Light has dawned" (Matthew 4:16). The Cane Ridge Revival would set America on fire and birth the Second Great Awakening.

HAMPTON-SYDNEY ACADEMY REVIVAL

In the decades leading up to the Cane Ridge Camp meeting, God was at work among the Presbyterians. Sparks of revival were beginning to be witnessed.

In 1787, John Blair Smith was installed as the President of the Hampton-Sydney Academy in Farmville, Virginia. Besides his educational and administrative responsibilities, he worked with local congregations. As he engaged the people, he found them "dull and lifeless." Sadly, his college students were even worse. None of his eighty students were "serious and thoughtful" about religion. Some even disparaged the Church.

Through intense prayer, Smith was quickened to counteract this trend. He organized prayer circles in the college and congregations. He guided them and taught them how to pray for revival. It was arduous work but soon their hearts grew warm.

Soon, many met frequently to pray for revival. By the summer of 1787, tremors were being felt among the students. Spiritual fervency ignited in a small group who became the catalyst for awakening. They aroused the other students, and in the fall, a revival swept through Hampton-Sydney Academy! As Smith and his assistants preached, students responded and they uttered unceasing prayers across the campus.

Before the end of the year, the students were taking the fire of revival back to their families and the congregations back home. The story of the miraculous transformation that happened at this college was the single most powerful stimulus for local revivals.

By the summer of 1788, Presbyterian congregations throughout Southern Virginia had been affected. News of the "Hampton-Sydney Revival" attracted visitors from Virginia and the Carolinas. Over the next three years, the revival spread to surrounding areas— even touching Baptists and Methodists.

In a dark and hopeless time, God was working through the Presbyterians. Among their ranks, heaven brought forth "flames of fire" (Psalm 104:4). Chosen men of God emerged who became known as the "Five Wild Men of the Cumberland"–James McGready, William Hodge, William McAdow, John Rankin, and Barton W. Stone. These men were devout Presbyterians, but impassioned Methodists and Baptists would later join them.

JAMES MCGREADY

Drawing on the same fire that stirred the Hampton-Sydney Academy, James McGready became a catalyst for revival in Kentucky. This evangelist preached fiery messages that awakened hearts in Logan County. With a coarse, loud voice, McGready held listeners spellbound. Sparks ignited across the southern and western parts of the state.

He was ultimately installed as the pastor in three rural congregations—the Red River, Gasper River, and Muddy River Churches. One of his listeners would later proclaim, "My mind was chained by him, and followed him closely in his rounds of heaven and earth, and hell with feelings indescribable."

The heavenly intervention became unmistakable in Logan and Christian county, near the waters of the Gasper and Red River. No one expected that the Presbyterian Communion meetings in the summer of 1800 would turn into a revival.

The Presbyterian communion services were widely attended as distant members and their families gathered together. It wasn't unusual for the gathering to turn into three-day affairs. Without adequate lodging, people would camp on the church grounds.

Though hundreds attended the communion service, only a few could receive the elements. Pastors would determine who was "worthy" and give them a "token" that allowed them to take part. This was called "Fencing of the Table." Nevertheless, all who gathered heard about the significance of the "Lord's Supper" and the warnings of the dire consequences of coming to the table without a pure heart.

In 1800, McGready invited his congregation and other local ministers to take part in the communion gathering at the Red River Church. William McGee, who was a fellow Presbyterian pastor joined him and he also brought his brother John who was a Methodist. They joined other dignitaries.

In the gathering, Friday, Saturday, and Sunday were relatively quiet—like conventional communion services. But on Monday, things shook loose. A woman who sought the assurance of salvation began shouting and singing. Aghast, most of the visiting Presbyterian ministers walked out. The McGee brothers, however, remained. William sat on the floor weeping, and thereafter, the entire congregation wept.

In his Methodist zeal, John stood up and exhorted the people to let "the Lord omnipotent reign in their hearts and to submit to Him." The congregants shouted and cried even louder. A wail of anguish cut through the air.

John, full of the Spirit, made his way to comfort the congregants when his brother reminded him that this was a Presbyterian church. They would never condone displays of emotionalism! But it was too late to stop the move of the Spirit. John later recalled what he experienced in that moment:

"I turned to go back and was near falling; the power of God was strong upon me. I turned again and, losing sight of the fear of man, I went through the place shouting and exhorting with all possible ecstasy and energy and the floor was soon filled with the slain."

Although these kinds of displays had been frowned upon by the Presbyterians, McGready and his associates were convinced this was the work of God. He laid plans for another sacramental service the following month. This outpouring of God spread like a flood. One participant said,

"The news of the strange operations which had transpired at the previous meeting had run throughout the country in every direction, carrying a high degree of excitement to the minds of almost every character."

The Gasper River congregation hosted the next communion service. On the first day of the gathering hundreds arrived from the surrounding region, ready to camp on the grounds.

The opening meetings were conventional, but the next day things erupted. By that evening, many were praying and crying for mercy—with hundreds lying powerless in the dirt. Few slept as ministers consoled desperate people throughout the night. Groans punctuated the Sunday morning communion service.

As the services closed out, the cries of the distressed overwhelmed the sound of the preaching. This prompted McGready to write: "After the congregation was dismissed… no person seemed to wish to go home—hunger and sleep seemed to affect nobody—eternal things were the vast concern."

THE RUMBLINGS OF REVIVAL

As 1800 drew to a close, the weather became cold. It became too frigid to have outdoor gatherings. But that didn't dilute the fervor. John McGee reported the stirrings of God that took place at the Desha's Creek Church, "The power of God was manifested. The people fell before the word, like corn before a storm of wind, and many rose from the floor with divine glory shining on their countenances."

Moving into the following year, the stirring of revivals were apparent in many parts of Kentucky. The McGee brothers, James McGready, and other "Wild Men of the Cumberland" continued to witness the power of God. These men were witnessing the rumblings of revival!

April 1801—Mason County Camp meeting:

"People began to be affected in very strange ways… weeping… trembling… wailing in apparent agony for their souls. The news of these strange spiritual operations, as they called them, spread and attracted people from all around to witness this power of God."

May 22, 1801—Cabin Creek Meeting:

"Lasting four days and three nights with loud exclamations of prayer and exhortations, people falling and crying for mercy, some struck with terror and others while running to escape were struck down in repentance by a supernatural power, others shouting and rejoicing."

June 1, 1801—Concord, Kentucky Camp meeting:

"Over 4000 attended. The meeting lasted five days and nights with a stunning move of the Spirit. No class, sex nor color, nor description was exempted. The Spirit fell on everyone from the age of eight months to ninety years."

July 1801—Pleasant Point, Kentucky:

"This meeting equaled if not surpassed any meeting that had been held up to that point."

July 24, 1801—Indian Creek in Harrison County:

"This meeting lasted five days and five nights. A twelve-year-old boy jumped on a tree stump and preached for about an hour..." at that moment the crowd fell like those who are shot in battle... in a manner which human language cannot describe."

THE CANE RIDGE CAMPMEETING

The revival at Hampton-Sydney Academy and other frontier stirrings were a prelude to an event that would transform the frontier—the Cane Ridge Camp meeting. Decades after this historic gathering, thousands still talked about what God did in the woods in Bourbon County, Kentucky. They would remember the blazing fire that launched the Second Great Awakening.

Barton W. Stone, the Presbyterian pastor in Cane Ridge, Kentucky, organized a communion service like what occurred at the Gasper and Red River. When he first began planning this event, he did not know how many would come. He wasn't trying to have a massive outdoor service; he wanted his congregation and people in the surrounding areas to experience the presence of God.

The Cane Ridge meetinghouse was on the slope of a hill surrounded by trees and bamboo—or cane from which the community derived its name. Surrounding the log edifice were pastures and spacious open grounds. This sanctuary had a large loft built over the first floor that enabled five hundred to be seated. Knowing that many would be coming, Stone and church members erected a tent. But they wondered if that would be enough. It wouldn't be. Over the next several days, as many as 30,000 converged in rural Kentucky.

On Friday, August 6, 1801, the meetinghouse was packed and the fields were covered. One witness counted over 140 wagons, fifty five wheeled carriages, and over 5000 horses and mules. In addition, a sea of tents covered the area. As Stone witnessed the crowds, he was astounded. People kept coming even though rain fell in torrents.

Stone made an opening address and thanked the people for gathering. Although the air was thick with expectancy, nothing extraordinary had taken place. Many of the seekers lingered all night in prayer. In many ways, Friday was the lull before the storm.

By Saturday, things changed. As far as the eye could see, one could witness families seeking the face of God. With so many, it was difficult to have only one preacher, so dozens of ministers climbed up on tree stumps, wagons, or horses to preach to the crowds. Although many of the ministers were Presbyterian, the Methodists and Baptists joined them as well.

In one part of the large encampment you could hear shouts and prayers. In another you could hear people singing hymns. Things started out as a minor earthquake and then built into a full-fledged tidal wave of power as the heavens were torn and the Holy Spirit came down. The wind swept over the pasture like a hurricane. James McGready wrote:

"The cries of the distressed arose almost as loud as the preacher's voices. Here awakening and converting work was to be found in every part of the multitude...sober Professors and high ranking Religious hierarchy were lying prostrate on the ground . . . multitudes in extreme stress . . . baffled description . . . many fell down as men slain in battle and stayed that way apparently breathless and motionless."

The Holy Spirit was free to move and thousands fell to the ground in trance-like states. Their pulse and breath were carefully monitored, and in many cases, it was hard to tell whether they were alive or dead. They called some medical personnel to restore consciousness. Some lay only for minutes, but others remained out in the Spirit for hours, and some even days. Some who had collapsed under the weight of God's glory were carried out and placed under trees for their protection. Eventually all rose up in joy.

As some encountered the presence of God, they rolled around in the dirt, crying out for mercy. The term "Holy Roller" was first used in the Second Great Awakening—not the Pentecostal meetings a century later. Overcome with divine power, many shook uncontrollably. In fact, a new denomination would later emerge from the revival—the *Shakers*.

An eyewitness account from the Cane Ridge Revival was handed down to us from an unbeliever. Shortly after he was touched by the revival, he became a minister of the gospel. James Finley wrote,

> In the month of August 1801, I learned there was to be a great meeting at Cane Ridge...feeling a great desire to see the wonderful things which had come to my ears...I resolved to go...If I fall it must be by physical power and not by singing or praying...and as I prided myself upon my manhood and courage, I had no fear...or being frightened into religion. I arrived upon the ground and here a scene presented itself to my mind not only novel and unaccountable, but awful beyond description...a vast crowd, supposed by some to have amounted to twenty-five thousand...the noise was like the roar of Niagara. The vast sea of human beings seemed to be agitated as if by a storm. I counted seven ministers, all preaching at one time, some on stumps, others in wagons, and one... was standing on a tree which had, in falling, lodged against another. Some people were singing, others praying, some crying for mercy... while others were shouting most vociferously...a peculiar strange sensation,

which I have never felt before, came over me. My heart beat tumultuously, my knees trembled, my lip quivered, and I felt as though I must fall to the ground. A strange supernatural power seemed to pervade the entire mass of my mind...I became so weak and powerless that I found it necessary to sit down. Soon after, I left and went deep into the woods and there I strove to rally my strength and man up my courage...after some time I returned to the scene of excitement, the waves of which, if possible, had risen still higher. The same...feeling came over me. I stepped up on a log so I could have a better view...the scene that then presented itself to my mind was indescribable. At one time I saw at least five hundred swept down in a moment, as if a battery of a thousand guns had been opened up on them, and then immediately followed shrieks and shouts that rent the very heavens, my whole frame trembled, my blood ran cold in my veins, and I fled for the woods a second time, and wished I had stayed at home...a sense of suffocation and blindness seemed to come over me...I thought I was going to die. There being a tavern about half a mile off, I concluded to go and get some brandy and see if it would strengthen my nerves... here I saw about one hundred men engaged in drunken revelry...I got to the bar and took a drink and left, feeling I was as near hell as I wished to be, either in this or the world to come...As soon as day broke I went to the woods to pray, and no sooner had my knees touched the ground than I cried for mercy and salvation, and fell prostate... suddenly my load was gone, my guilt removed...and the direct witness from heaven shone full upon my soul...I cried, I laughed, I shouted, and so strangely did I appear to all . . . that they thought me deranged."

All kinds of unusual phenomenon and activity was taking place. Fifty drunk ruffians decided to come out to the camp meeting site and cause trouble. The foul men mounted their horses and raced toward the crowd at a full gallop. They intended to cause havoc and stir reactions. However, as the horses neared the crowds, they came to a complete stop. It was as though they ran into an invisible angelic wall. The drunkards were thrown off the backs of the horses. With sprained necks and broken bones, their cries of anguish rose in sync with the cries of adoration and exhortations from the crowd.

The countryside was aflame and word spread like wildfire. Hour after hour, people arrived who heard of this great move of God. Far and wide over a one hundred-mile radius, they came with anticipation and expectation to witness the wondrous things that God was doing. One prominent minister said he had made an accurate count of three thousand souls on the ground as if dead.

They held the Sunday Communion Service in relative calm inside the meeting house, but outside was a different story. With little sleep, fatigued ministers were exhorting sinner and saint alike. One preached perched fifteen feet above the ground, standing on a fallen tree. Sinners were dropping down, shrieking, groaning, crying for mercy. Others, with inexpressible joy on their faces, were hugging and kissing each other, speaking in incoherent sentences [tongues] or wracked by uncontrollable laughter.

A seven-year-old girl sitting on her father's shoulder was completely exhausted. When she lowered her head to sleep, someone in the crowd said, "the poor thing had better be laid down to rest." The girl lifted her head and exclaimed," Do not call me poor, for Christ is my brother, God my father, and I have a Kingdom to inherit, and therefore do not call me poor, for I am rich in the blood of the Lamb." Those in the crowd were flabergasted by the authority that she spoke in.

By Monday, food and supplies were running short, forcing several families to head home. As they left, others were just arriving because they had just heard of the revival. People continued to flood the grounds, and the excitement continued.

The sound astonished the newcomers. Many could not believe the sheer level of noise. It was said that people traveling to the revival could hear the roar at great distances away. Ministers were weary, but continued to help the individuals that were in turmoil. Finally, some of them with no voice left to preach, retired to the meetinghouse to sleep or dropped to the ground in complete exhaustion.

For four more days, the singing, praying, preaching, and manifestations continued. But things slowly ebbing to a stop on Thursday, August 12. So many were overwhelmed by what occurred. Barton Stone made the following declaration: "A particular description of this meeting would fill a large volume, and then half would not be told."

THE AFTERMATH

The Cane Ridge Revival ended, but the overwhelming presence of God that the participants of the camp meeting encountered lingered long afterward.

A mighty awakening had rescued America from the brink of deep darkness. Afterward, holy enthusiasm spread from Kentucky to the other parts of the frontier, and to the whole nation.

A year later, a man traveling to Lexington reported that people everywhere still talked about "little else but the great revival of religion." The anointing was so strong that he proclaimed, "I had felt much anxiety lest I should fall down when amongst them."

Do it again, Lord, do it again!

"When I saw Him, I fell at His feet as if I were dead" (Revelation 1:16).

6

THE HAWAIIAN AWAKENING

Hawaiian Prayer Meeting

"The power of God seemed to descend on the assembly 'like a rushing mighty wind' and…bore all down before it. I stood amazed at the influence that seized the audience almost universally and could compare it to nothing more aptly than the irresistible force of a mighty torrent." —David Brainerd

"One of the problems with describing what God has done in history is that He is still alive and writing it." —Winkie Pratney

"May God increase our spiritual hunger to see Him bless our churches again with great spiritual renewal. May He bless our nation again with mighty spiritual awakenings. God is the God of revival." —Wesley Duewel

"I will also give You as a light to the Gentiles, That you should be my salvation to the ends of the earth." —Isaiah (49:6)

"Whole days and weeks have I spent prostrate on the ground in silent or vocal prayer." —George Whitefield

Although the Hawaiian Islands were a testament to God's beauty, for centuries, they were shrouded in darkness. Idolatry, human sacrifice, and sexual immorality were rooted in their way of life. The people were blind to the ways of Christ.

Evil had gripped the islands for centuries, but in the early nineteenth century, God sovereignly moved. A land entangled in wickedness and perversion experienced the gospel. Titus Coan, a missionary in the Pacific islands said,

"Many listened with tears, and after preaching, when I supposed they would return to their homes and give me rest, they remained and gathered around me so earnestly that I had no time to eat. And in places where I spent my nights they filled the house to its entire capacity, leaving scores outside who could not enter."

Coan's report was shocking to Christian leaders in the United States and Europe. Many pastors overlooked these islanders, believing that they could never be saved. They knew that the Hawaiians offered human beings to pagan gods—throwing babies into volcanoes. Most could sense that the principalities and powers of darkness ruled the islands. There was evidence of wickedness throughout their society.

For centuries, there was no semblance of family in Hawaii. Children roamed the countryside; left to fend for themselves. With loose bonds in tribes, sexual immorality and perversion became common. Innocent children weren't valued. Most women became childless because of their cultural infanticide. They cut down the population by tens of thousands. Untold numbers of young people had been sacrificed to wicked gods.

In the nineteenth century, a high priest and priestess ruled the islands. This wicked overlord was 6'5 and was a vile man—a drunkard, a thief, an adulterer, and a murderer. His sister, the priestess, had the same reputation. When they weren't pursuing their own abhorrent interests, they tried to appease "Pele," the volcano goddess, with human sacrifices. Human flesh was being offered up daily.

What happened to cause such a sovereign move of God to change such degradation in the hearts of these pagans? God, who rules over the affairs of mankind started putting the pieces together decades before this awakening happened. Let us go back a decade earlier to another part of the world and see the handiwork, the wisdom, knowledge, and judgments of God.

TITUS COAN

In the 1820s, the Second Great Awakening covered America like a blanket. It was a time of evangelical fervor and revival within the established churches and an awakening of conviction and repentance among the unbelievers. It wasn't just one or two people getting saved at a time, but entire neighborhoods. Thousands of conversions were being reported.

The intensity of revivals in New York and New England created areas nicknamed "The Burned-Over Districts" because the spiritual fervor was so high it seemed to set the places on fire. Many were powerfully impacted through these meetings.

Titus Coan (1801-1882) spent his mid-twenties immersed in the revivals that were sweeping New England under Asahel Nettleton and Charles Finney. Being acquainted with both revivalists, he learned how to walk, preach, and maintain the "moving of the Spirit." For a short time, Coan labored alongside Finney. He was amazed, watching a lifeless congregation suddenly became a mass of broken, convicted humanity. Those who had been hard-hearted were blubbering, rolling, and crawling on the floor in distress for their souls. As he served in these revivals, he never imagined God would call him to touch the lives of people 5400 miles away.

MISSIONARIES TO HAWAII

After a short courtship of a woman named Fidelia Church, Coan married her in 1834 and boarded a ship to what they then called the Sandwich Islands. We now know them as Hawaii.

The Coans were not the first American missionaries to bring the gospel to this land. Hiram and Sybil Bingham preceded them in 1820. But a work had already been in progress through some Tahitian evangelists who had traveled there decades before. Although some strongholds of idolatry and pagan taboos had been brought down, the pre-existing work only had minimal success. The Tahitian effort was less adapted to facilitate the work of the Holy Spirit. A harsher form of Calvinism had characterized their preaching.

Bingham and leaders from the seventeen churches on the archipelago prayed for an earth-shaking revival. But while they were looking upward for the Spirit to come down, God sent a humble man to bring his message of grace—Titus Coan.

Coan and his wife arrived in the Pacific islands with a whole different temperament and anointing. They understood the message of mercy and love. God would use them to counteract the darkness.

The experiences that Coan had in the earlier revival meetings in the Burned-Over Districts quickened his faith. Coan believed that the Holy Spirit would turn the archipelago upside down with every island being brought under the authority of the kingdom of God. This hope that was building in him was essential because the Haili Church where he was installed as pastor had only twenty-three members. Coan would need to have God's favor to succeed. With his intercession and relentless pursuit of Christ, Hawaii would undergo a transformation that has rarely been seen.

Other anointed missionaries joined Coan in his revival efforts — Sheldon Dibble, Lorenzo Lyons, and Lowell Smith. People called them, "The Four Horsemen of Revival." S. E. Bishop writes, in the March 1902 issue of "The Friend,"

> "The entrance of these devoted men into the Hawaiian work gave a new impulse to the evangelization of the people. There was a more direct and efficient presentation of Christ . . . less encumbered by old and stiff... forms of doctrine. This new preaching undoubtedly contributed much to the great spiritual awakening among the Hawaiians."

Months later, Bishop wrote that the four were embodiments of the fire-breathed Finney revivals in America: "[The] missionaries who experienced the Charles G. Finney revivals in New York are, Dibble, Coan, Lyons, and Lowell Smith, whose souls had felt the peculiar kindling of the Spirit and who brought with them His peculiar flame."

Coan labored to replicate the fervor of the Finney revivals while he ministered to the Hawaiians. He discovered that "like doctrines, prayers and efforts seemed to produce like fruits." What became clear in his missions effort was the relationship between fervent, intercessory prayer and revival. Coan wrote,

> "Prayer is an essential link in the chain of causes that lead to a revival, as much as truth is. Some have zealously used bible truth to convert men and laid very little stress on prayer. They have preached, and talked, and distributed tracts with great zeal, and then wondered that they had so little success. And the reason was that they forgot to use the other branch of the means, effectual prayer. They overlooked the fact that truth, by itself, will never produce the effect, without the Spirit of God, and that Spirit is given in answer to prayer."

After arriving on the Islands, Coan labored to learn the native language. But even before gaining fluency, his English exhortations still impacted the people. Although they couldn't understand what he was saying, they still felt drawn in. Coan wanted to emulate Christ. While among the people, he had a "personal magnetism of love" that drew all "sweetly and irresistibly, to the Love of God in Christ." In a letter to colleagues Coan wrote:

> "When I came to these islands, and before I could use the Hawaiian language, I often felt as if I should burst with a strong desire to speak the word to the surrounding natives. And when my mouth was opened to speak of the love of God in Christ, in my own language, I felt that the very chords of my heart were wrapped around my hearers, and that some... power was helping me to draw them in, as the fisherman feels when drawing in his net filled with fishes."

PREVAILING PRAYER

Historians who recorded what transpired during the Hawaiian Awakening were struck by the intense emphasis on prayer. The missionaries were interceding and sending requests to the United States on behalf of the Sandwich Islands. At the same time Hawaiian converts gave themselves, wholeheartedly, to prevailing prayer others were praying for them. One missionary wrote, "A number were in the habit of rising an hour before light and resorting to the school house to pray for the coming of the Holy Spirit."

A blind Hawaiian preacher, Puaaiki, known as the "Blind Preacher of Maui," asked believers to give themselves to prevailing prayer. This type of intercession was unique in that era because it was unified, focused, and loud. Each person would cry out to God at the same time. At that time, most Western Christians embraced a quiet, solemn spirituality. Because of their preference for the silent, meditative approach, many missionaries were uncomfortable with the fiery intercession. They didn't like how the Hawaiians were praying, but they could not deny the results. One report declared, "Missionaries declare that they had never witnessed more earnest, humble, persevering wrestling in prayer, than was exhibited . . . at this time."

People from every walk of life were being impacted. Age made no difference. A reporter noted, "One could scarcely go in any direction, in the sugar-cane or banana groves, without finding children praying and weeping before God."

This type of bold prayer was impacting people not even on the Islands. A group of missionaries, traveling on a ship from Boston with supplies for the Islands, prayed every morning and evening. On the open seas, revival broke out aboard ship. Soon the Captain, officers, and crew made a public commitment to Christ.

REVIVAL FIRE FALLS

By November 1836, Coan felt that he was fluent enough in the Hawaiian language to preach without interpreters. So, he launched his first preaching tour of Hawaii on foot. Coan declared the glorious fire of revival to sixteen thousand souls from 100 miles around the church. He labored for thirty days before he saw the fruit of all the fervent revival praying that his congregation had been conducting.

Suddenly, all of Hawaii was in an outpouring of the Holy Spirit. It wasn't just in one place. It swept all the islands at once. Coan wrote:

"I preached three, four, five times a day . . . The people rallied in masses and were eager to hear the Word. Many listened with tears and after the preaching. When I supposed they would return home and give me rest, they remained and crowded around me so earnestly that I had no time to eat. In places where I spent nights, they filled the house to its entire capacity, leaving scores outside who could not enter. All wanted to hear more of the word of Life."

The people would press in and try to receive from Coan until long after midnight, and the work would resume at the crack of dawn. The islanders were swept off their feet when Coan spoke, overcome with an insatiable hunger for God. Coan writes,

"From the time I arrived in Kau, until I reached home, a period of eight days, I preached forty-three times. And often to congregations that listened with much interest and many tears... hundreds of natives pressed upon me afterward to receive instruction... There was so much interest that I found myself preaching three times before breakfast, which I ate at ten o'clock. I could not move out of doors, in any direction, without being thronged by people from all sides, who could find no other opportunity to converse with me (about Christ). Some followed me from village to village to hear the gospel. Many were pricked in their hearts and asked what they should do to be saved."

One of the most wonderful testimonies of God's awesome power was in the transformation of the wicked High Priest who lived near the volcano. After listening to Coan preach God's word, he fell to the ground in repentance, weeping and seeking forgiveness. Years later, he was still an active member of the Hilo congregation.

Coan returned to Hilo, and natives came from miles away to hear him preach the Bible. Hundreds left far-flung villages and relocated less a mile from the church. So many islanders were giving their lives to Christ that he needed to institute a follow-up system to keep track of all the converts:

"I had a faithful notebook in my pocket, and in all my personal conversations with the people, by night and by day, at home and in my oft repeated tours, I had noted down, unobserved, the names of individuals apparently sincere and true converts. Over these persons I kept watch, though unconsciously to themselves; and thus their life and conversations were made the subjects of vigilant observation. After a lapse of... six, nine, or twelve months... selections were made... for examination. Some were found to have gone back to their old sins... while many had stood fast and run well."

When on preaching tours, he would take his record book with him so he could check up on church members in nearby villages. Coan wrote, "When anyone did not answer the roll call, I made inquiry why. If dead, I marked the date; if sick, visited him or her; . . . if absent on duty, accepted the fact; if supposed to be doubting or backsliding, sent for or visited him."

Within six months, thousands were brought into the church. The revival had become such an overwhelming move of the sovereign God that it was now considered "Hawaii's Great Awakening."

The Hawaiians hungered for righteousness, and repentance of sin was openly expressed. Coan reports that once, while he was holding an outdoor meeting in Puna, one man burst out in tears and travail in the middle of the sermon. He cried, "Lord, have mercy on me; I am dead in sin." This new convert's weeping was so loud and trembling so great that he moved the entire congregation to their knees. One witness wrote, "The scene was such as I had never before witnessed. I stood dumb in the midst of this weeping, watching, praying multitudes, not being able to make myself heard for about twenty minutes."

This kind of response became a common practice in the revival meetings as God rent the heavens. The Holy Spirit was convicting the islanders of sin, righteousness, and judgment. Coan shared the following report:

> "I arrived yesterday at 8:00 A.M. found a large company of children... in the meeting houses besides several hundreds of adults. I was a little weary, but I felt the Spirit break upon my heart; so I went right in among the children and fell on my knees and looked up to heaven. The Holy Spirit fell instantly, soon as I opened my mouth. The place was shaken. The congregation was all in tears, and there was such a crying out as I had not heard before."

There was no escaping the conviction of the Holy Spirit. His presence permeated every corner of the islands. Wherever missionaries spoke the word of God, everyone listening would be shaken. Their muscles quivered, and they fell by the hundreds in "tremendous throes" like a "dying giant or broken down with an earthquake shock . . . groaning on the ground for fifteen minutes or half an hour."

Many of the unrighteous attempted to escape, but wherever they hid, the Holy Spirit manifested and overpowered them. Coan describes this heaven-sent hunger:

> "There were places along the routes where there were no houses near the trail, but where a few families were living a half mile or more inland. In such places, the few dwellers would come down the path leading their blind, and carrying their sick and aged upon their backs, and lay them down under a tree if there was one near, or upon the naked rocks, that they might hear of a Savior. It was often affecting to see those withered and trembling hands reach out to grasp the hand of the teacher, and to hear the palsied, the blind, and the lame begging him to stop awhile and tell them the story of Jesus."

This was God! Over three-quarters of the island population surrendered to the Lord of Hosts! Island to island everywhere you looked, knees were bowed before the "Lamb who took away the sin of the world." People could not get enough of God. Sleep was impossible as the yearning intensified. One contemporary shared the following:

> "The town of Hilo swelled to ten times its original size, growing from 1,000 people to 10,000. This was due to people moving in from outlining areas so they could attend church and hear God's word."

They rang bells in villages to let the people know that the preaching of the word was about to transpire. No matter what time of the day it was rung, three to six thousand would gather within a short time.

Coan trained his converts in the ways of God. He would send

out church members from Hilo two by two to preach throughout the parish. Coan wrote, "They… went out two by two into all the villages, exhorting, persuading, weeping, and praying… with these helpers every village became a guarded citadel of the Lord."

As God moved through the villages, people gave their lives to God and got rid of their idols. Darkness was being pushed back.

The islanders not only embraced Jesus, they surrendered all of their lives and possessions. They held nothing back from the Lord of the Harvest. John Wesley once said, "The last thing that is converted in a man is his purse." Real revival transforms everything. The Hawaiian converts loathed the thought of going to church empty handed. Though destitute, they gave vegetables, salt, fish, eggs, coconuts, birds, and fire wood. If they had nothing else, they were ready to offer their time and labor.

Amid the surging revival, the islanders had a tremendous hunger for the Word of God. So Coan and others helped initiate the printing of native language Bibles. They gave the first copy to Queen Kaahumanu on her death bed.

The work of God in the awakening showed up in multiple ways including supernatural protection. The Hilo believers were so devout that, under the leading of the Lord, they left town to participate in a prayer meeting. While the town was deserted, on November 7, 1837, a tsunami struck. If they had not gone inland, they would have died. Coan wrote,

> "Had this catastrophe occurred after midnight when all were asleep, hundreds of lives would . . . have been lost . . . Only thirteen were drowned . . . the dead were buried; fed, comforted and clothed the living, and God brought light out of darkness, joy out of grief, and life out of death… our meetings were more and more crowded, and hopeful converts were multiplied."

Light came amid darkness. In all the revival meetings, a "token of the Holy Spirit" was common. People encountered wails, shrieks, and participants falling to the ground unconscious. This overwhelming sense of God's presence affected young and old.

Except for Coan's friends and colleagues, missionaries on the islands did not understand the manifestations of the Holy Spirit. Nevertheless, they knew that God's Hand was leading and guiding the awakening. One reluctantly acknowledged, "to doubt that it was the work of the Spirit, was to grieve the Holy Spirit and provoke Him to depart from us."

Coan was criticized in some circles for allowing the services to be interrupted by shaking and emotional outbursts. He rebuffed these criticisms with the undeniable evidence that the manifestations always brought "genuine repentance." He made it clear, "he wasn't going to put them down."

So many miracles and unusual displays transpired in the meetings. People were having experiences like the believers in the early Church. One report shared the following testimony:

"A young man came once into our meeting to make sport slyly. Trying to make the young men around him laugh during prayer, he fell as senseless as a log upon the ground and was carried out of the house. It was sometime before his consciousness would be restored. He became sober, confessed his sins, and in due time united with the church."

Coan would share some of the things that he witnessed from time to time. In one report, he said,

"I would rise before the restless, noisy crowd and begin (preaching). It wasn't long before I felt I had got hold of them. There seemed to be a chord of electricity binding them to me. I know that I had them, that they would not go away. The Spirit would hush them by the truth till they would sob and cry, 'What shall we do?' and the noise of the weeping would be so great that I could not go on."

Hiram Bingham, the missionary who worked alongside Coan, spoke of the wonderment of the movement and anointing of the Holy Spirit over the people. He wrote,

> "Indeed, there was a shaking among the dry ones throughout the nation. The Spirit of God most manifestly hovered over the islands… Thousands of the liberated appeared to be coming to Zion and celebrating the praises of the Deliverer… This gracious visitation of the Spirit of God from on high led unusual thousands to crowd the doors of the sanctuaries… where the united cry of many ascended into heaven."

So many demonstrations of power transpired that it would take volumes to adequately report them. Suffice it to say, Hawaii's "Great Awakening" was a modern day "Book of Acts."

The awakening transformed a nation. Tens of thousands came to the Lord. The light and glory of the gospel had overtaken the islands. Hawaii became a Christian nation. In a public speech, King Kamehameha III reflected on the islands' character. He said, "The life of the land is preserved in righteousness." The legal code of Hawaii was changed to reflect their new found Christian faith: "The religion of the Lord Jesus Christ shall continue to be the established national religion of the Hawaiian Islands."

Hawaiian missionaries set out to spread the gospel across the inhabited Pacific islands. The ministry team carried a letter of greeting from King Kamehameha III to the Caroline Islands. The Christian monarch's goal was to graciously persuade a neighboring nation to "renounce their idols and worship the true and living God."

A WARNING

After several years of fervor, the revival waned in the 1840s. There were several factors contributing to this. One of which was "foreign diseases." A Californian cargo ship, docked in Hilo Bay, contributed to a terrible measles epidemic. Around 10,000 Hawaiians died from this outbreak. Later foreign merchants carried the small pox virus. Thousands more died because of this. Those who remained were fearful and distracted.

Despite the problems, God kept moving in Hawaii. Yet, within the free movement of the Holy Spirit, evil men found opportunities to creep in. Many wanted to take advantage of the generosity and openness of the islanders.

Sectarian religious denominations infiltrated the islands, confusing the people and turning them away from the deeper work of the Holy Spirit. Before long, missionaries from Episcopal, Roman Catholic, and Mormon institutions established bases on Hawaii. They spread dissension and broke up the unity of the Spirit.

Coan's heart was broken. He said,

> "Our Hawaiian churches are not called Episcopal, Presbyterian, or Congregational, or by any other name than that of the Great Head, the Shepherd, and Bishop of souls. We call them 'Christian Churches' . . . Controversies among Christians always sadden me. Our warfare is against sin and Satan; and heaven's 'sacramental host' (the body of Christ) should never fall out by the way, or spend an hour in their conflict with hell, fighting one another . . . the whole Church of Christ should clasp hands and march shoulder to shoulder against the common foe."

Another factor that hindered the revival was the rise of the sugar industry. The money-grubbing merchants brought in cheap foreign laborers from China and Japan. These men, with their pagan beliefs and customs, soon outnumbered the Hawaiian Christians.

Even as the awakening ebbed, Titus Coan never stopped laboring for Jesus. Besides many evangelistic efforts, he worked toward building a congregation in Haili and establishing six others in Hilo. Coan was restless in his efforts to advance the gospel.

A FRESH OUTBREAK

His unrelenting efforts resulted in a fresh outbreak of revival in 1860-1861. Thousands of backslidden believers returned to the Lord with renewed zeal. They held services three times per day, often lasting until after midnight. Prayer meetings were erupting throughout the islands with an intensity that eclipsed the intercession of the "Great Awakening" decades earlier. The laborers brought in from other parts of Asia to labor in the sugar industry were now being affected by the gospel. They renounced Buddhism and worshipped the one true God.

Intercession and prayer, under the efforts of Titus Coan, transformed a land that was once gripped by darkness.

> "Now when the Gentiles heard this, they were glad and glorified the word of the Lord. And as many as had been appointed to eternal life believed" (Acts 13:48).

7

ROBERT CLEAVER CHAPMAN

Robert Cleaver Chapman

"When considering your faults and inclined to dejection concerning them, don't talk with yourself, you will be keeping bad company. Talk with the Lord." —William Hake

"Be perfect as your Father in heaven is perfect." —Jesus
Christ (Mathew 5:4)

"Discernment is God's call to intercession never to faultfinding."
—Corrie Ten Boom

"Let us give our week, our thoughts, our plans, ourselves, our
lives, our loved ones, our influence, our all, right into His hand,
and then, when all have been given over to Him, there will be
nothing left for us to trouble about, or to make trouble about."
—Hudson Taylor

"There are many who preach Christ but not so many who live
Christ; my great aim will be to 'live' Christ."—Robert C.
Chapman

❧

Although not much of an orator, Robert Cleaver Chapman
(1803–1902) was known across Europe for his
unwavering compassion and devout prayer life. This humble
pastor, mostly forgotten in religious circles today, was one of the
most celebrated Christians of his generation.

Chapman lived simply, centering his life around intercession,
but his spirituality attracted multitudes. This impoverished
pastor was friends with several prominent figures, including
George Müller, John Nelson Darby, and James Hudson Taylor.
When asked about Chapman, Charles Haddon Spurgeon—the
prince of preachers—referred to him as "the saintliest man I ever
knew."

Hussey Burgh Macartney (1799-1894), an influential
Anglican clergyman, had heard much about Chapman, and
wondered if the tales were true. He visited the pastor in his
home in Barnstaple and later wrote,

"I learned that he was preeminently holy; a man who rose early, prayed much, and always walked with God... a visitor who had once been obliged to break in upon his solitude beheld his face as it had been the face of an angel."

Many of Chapman's contemporaries had good things to say about him, even if they differed in biblical interpretation. John Nelson Darby, a prominent Brethren Bible teacher, got into a doctrinal disagreement with Chapman. Darby took some liberties with scriptural readings that Chapman was unwilling to accept. This impasse frustrated the high-strung Darby. One can only imagine how angry he must have been. However, when Darby later heard others criticizing Chapman, he wouldn't stand for it. Abruptly interrupting their diatribe, he said, "You leave that man alone; he lives what I teach . . . We talk about heavenly places, but Robert Chapman lives in them." Even those who disagreed with this devout man gave him honor.

Chapman's life has even arrested the attention of historians. Contemplating this praying pastor's influence, one researcher acknowledged:

"The modern Christian, looking back upon the life of Chapman from a distance of some years, may well ponder whether God has not given us the example of such a life to serve as a witness to the true nature of New Testament Christianity."

Chapman's devout faith and unwavering devotion has been inspiring to a multitude of believers. A modern biographer reiterates that Chapman

"shines out above all parties and differences, as a man of God loving, but uncompromising; gentle, but searching; humble, but one who spoke with the authority; gifted, but utterly childlike; self-effacing, but never to be forgotten."

HUGGING HIS CHAINS

The godly intercessor and philanthropist that Chapman became was radically different from his beginnings.

Robert Cleaver Chapman was born into a wealthy family and bred to be a prominent figure in English society. From the time he was young, they sent him to the finest schools. He became fluent in six languages and was trained to weld influence on society.

As a young man, Chapman enrolled in law school. Though this profession could be distasteful, he wanted to hold on to wealth, prestige, and honor. Chapman would do whatever was necessary to remain a part of the elite circles in London.

The Church of England was a part of Chapman's life. However, it was more of a civic duty than the product of heartfelt faith. Chapman read the Bible and believed that it was true. But Jesus' message of grace had not penetrated his heart.

Chapman mistakenly believed salvation was gained through good works. Favor with God came through his own efforts. Chapman hoped that the good outweighed the bad. But it was hard to know. In time, his religious efforts felt like an exercise in futility. Chapman said,

> "I hugged my chains. I would not, could not, hear the voice of Jesus. My cup was bitter with my guilt and the fruit of my doings. Sick was I of the world, hating it in vexation of spirit, while yet I was unable and unwilling to cast it out."

Chapman was entangled in an intense spiritual struggle. Little did he know that his dull religious mindset was about to be upended.

DELAY NOT TO KEEP HIS COMMANDMENTS

James Harrington Evans, a former Anglican cleric, invited Chapman to attend a church service at the John Street Chapel in London. Though this fellowship remained a part of the Church of England, it was moving toward non-conformity. Chapman agreed to attend to appease his curiosity. He wanted to hear more about the so-called "heretical" views of Evans.

As Chapman attended, he was overwhelmed with the message of freedom. As the Holy Spirit came over him, the restrictions and distorted views of his denominational religiosity became clear. It appalled Chapman that he misunderstood the centrality of the gospel. With a pricked conscience and scriptural clarity, he entered into an intimate relationship with Jesus Christ by faith alone.

Chapman approached Evans and asked to be baptized. Since the pastor knew this zealous young man was newly sanctified, he said, "You will wait awhile, and consider the matter." Chapman replied, "No, I will make haste, and delay not, to keep His commandments!" So Evans made arrangements for him to be baptized right away.

The following Sunday, Chapman stood before the congregation at John Street Chapel, dressed in a sky blue, swallow-tailed coat, with large gilt buttons—the fashion of the well-to-do society. He was an upper class lawyer staring out at a room full of people in tattered every-day clothing. The societal differences could not be starker. But God was bringing together the rich and the poor for his glory.

As Chapman addressed the congregation, giving testimony to his conversion, his words astonished them. He said that since he accepted Christ, the gems of this world have grown strangely dim. Everyone could see that Jesus had done something amazing in Chapman's life.

While the non-conformists at John Street Chapel were

thrilled with Chapman's transformation, others didn't take it as well. His new religious stance bewildered some of his other colleagues. Some family members and his closest friends were enraged. How could he descend into the world of the weak and impoverished? With tears, Chapman wrote, even to "my own flesh and blood . . . I became a witness against them to my boasting only in Him."

BECOMING NOTHING TO WIN OTHERS TO CHRIST

Chapman continued in his legal occupation, as he grew in faith, and his career prospered. His reputation as a gracious, honest man and devout believer drew many clients to him. However, no longer attending the lavish banquets of the aristocrats, his status in London's well-to-do society drastically plummeted.

With the love of Jesus in his heart, Chapman no longer cared about the advantages of social prominence. He was now a part of something more majestic. He was doing the work of the sovereign King of heaven. Instead of banquets, Chapman was consumed with a desire to be as "nothing that he might win Christ."

Drawing from his amassed fortune, he ministered to the destitute, and those entangled in sin. He often spent his evenings with the poor in the ram shackle districts of the city. Even though he wasn't much of an orator, he continually preached the gospel of Christ. One of his listeners remarked, "even though he was a solicitor of the law, he was a poor preacher." This inability didn't stop Chapman. This was the reply that he made to that criticism: "There are many who preach Christ, but not so many who live Christ; my great aim will be to 'live' Christ." Although Chapman was a lawyer, he wasn't one in his heart. Things were rapidly changing for him. Chapman knew that if he was to represent Christ on earth, people would have to see the reality of the sacrificial Lamb through his life. He was dedicated to reflecting Christ, but to his dismay, finer things still had a pull on him. Chapman was willing to go low, but underneath it all, pride was still his "besetting sin."

To get where he needed to go, he knew that he had to jump off the top of the social ladder. Although he had been doing this for some time, he needed to go even lower. Chapman wrote,

> "Give yourself to attacking the filthiness of the spirit more than the filthiness of the flesh—pride, selfishness, self-seeking, etc.— these are the ringleaders; aim at them... while you are occupied in gaining the victory over little sins, great sins will be occupied in gaining victory over you. When the great sins are overcome, little sins fall with them."

Chapman realized that he had to forsake his fortune and the accolades of wealth. He needed to live like George Mueller, a ministry friend from Bristol who walked away from everything and depended on God. Mueller's faith inspired Chapman to move in the same direction.

So, Chapman gave up his wealth, along with all future pastoral income. He was determined, by prayer and faith, to rely on God for everything. Chapman wrote, "If people would come and live for a week or two in a household where the smallest item was received at God's Hand by faith, it would help them in their own lives."

As Chapman divested his wealth, the hardest luxury to give up was a chauffeur-driven coach. For decades, he was accustomed to being driven around the town by coachmen. Now, he had to go everywhere on foot. Chapman later jokingly quipped, "My pride never got over it."

He was utterly transformed as he gave everything over to Jesus. Discussing his new traveling arrangements with a friend, Chapman wrote, "I was obliged to use conveyances; but, oh!

How much rather do I choose to travel by foot for the work of the Lord, and communion with Him!"

EBENEZER STRICT BAPTIST CHAPEL

At twenty-nine, Chapman received an invitation to pastor at the Ebenezer Strict Baptist Chapel at Barnstaple. The congregants understood he was not eloquent when he preached, but they didn't mind. Chapman's holiness and separation from corruptible, worldly things were more than enough. They wanted a godly pastor.

While Chapman was non-sectarian, the Ebenezer Strict Baptist Chapel was on the opposite end of spectrum. As the name implied, they were strict Baptists—an extremely closed community that restricted membership. Many of this fellowship's values were in direct conflict with Chapman. Drawing from Galatians 5:1, the former lawyer believed that Christ offered freedom to every man. The text proclaims: "Stand fast therefore in the liberty by which Christ has set us free and do not be entangled again with the yoke of bondage."

In his biography of Chapman, Frank Holmes explores the reality of these conflicting views:

> "This text [Galatians 5:1]… undermined the Strict Baptist position completely, since they will only receive those who have been baptized by immersion on a profession of faith, and forbid the Lord's table and all fellowship, any who do not fill this condition, even though they have ample proof that Christ has accepted such as His people."

Although there were marked differences, Chapman was ready for the challenge. He told them he would accept their invitation to the pastorate, but only if they agreed with one condition. He would gladly serve them if he had freedom to teach the scriptures broadly and without being forced into their pre-exiting denominational slant. He said that he would not give credence to the hollow doctrines of men. Chapman wanted to let the scriptures have the full freedom to move and breathe.

Chapman didn't expect them to go along with his demand, but surprisingly, they agreed. With this, the door was opened for genuine scriptural engagement. There would be little restriction as the people wrestled the scriptures with their pastor. This new beginning would enable many wonderful things to enfold.

When Chapman first began teaching, the congregation was inclined to continue in their ingrained religious practices, but with time, they changed. He refused to entertain sectarian ideas such as the banishment of people from the fellowship.

Chapman said, as long as one believed on "the Lord Jesus Christ and Him crucified and that he is the Son of God and died and rose again as atonement for sin," they could be a part of the fellowship. He believed it was important to "receive one another, just as Christ also received us, to the glory of God" (Romans 15:7)

Denominationalism often had a grating sound to his ear. Chapman felt it was contrary to the identity and mission of the Church. Chapman believed that many of the beloved names, titles, and sectarian arguments were a tool of the enemy to keep Christians divided.

It was slow work, but, in time, Chapman and his "Strict Baptist" church entered into the fullness of the Spirit. He could expound on the scriptures with incredible authority, but with overwhelming humility. The church enjoyed tremendous fellowship and love. It drew many into what the Lord was doing.

Chapman's undying compassion for the people led to him being called the "Apostle of Love." Week after week, several unconverted individuals joined the church. People were coming to salvation, not because of Chapman's preaching, but because of the love of Christ emanating from him.

As many came through the doors, Chapman was eager to set the highest standard of honor. He did not like gossip or "tale-bearing." He was extremely gracious with his congregants, but this was a behavior that he despised. Whenever someone brought up the faults of others, he would interrupt them with the following: "Let us go to our brother and tell him of this."

One day, a woman of his church came to him and expressed distress about the conduct of another sister in the congregation. While she was still talking, he stood up and put on his overcoat. Startled, she said, "I came to you for advice." He replied, "I will give it, when you come with me to call on the sister," at which point, humbly, she confessed her lack of love.

Later, an argument erupted in the church and a group of people split from the fellowship. The breakaway party angrily demanded access to the church auditorium in order to meet twice a week. Chapman allowed them access to the building and said, "Just as I should give my coat to a man who demanded it." He referred to them as "Brethren dearly beloved and longed for, whose consciences led them to refuse my fellowship and to deprive me of theirs." Chapman was unique in his pastoral role. He gained a reputation as a man of compassion and grace.

BIBLE SMUGGLER AND HYMN WRITER

Chapman touched lives in other ways outside the pastorate. One way was through the composition of poems and hymns. This beloved pastor had quite a way with words and penned over one hundred and fifty heartfelt songs. Some of the hymns he wrote are still used today.

This devoted intercessor also conducted evangelistic campaigns in different locales. Even at an advanced age, Chapman maintained a regular open-air meeting schedule. The local newspaper editor respected Chapman and often printed his entire messages. His ministry touched many.

Sometimes Chapman conducted more extensive mission campaigns. In 1838, he visited Spain with another ministry team for an outreach. They took several Bibles and passed them out clandestinely. This was a risky enterprise because this practice was illegal.

In 1863 and 1871, Chapman returned to Spain with other missionaries. On his third trip, authorities arrested him for distributing bibles at a train depot. When Chapman was taken to the police station and questioned, he reached into his wallet, retrieved some money and asked, "Have I a right to throw this to the poor who beg at the station?" Then, holding a Bible high, he asked, "Here is bread; have I a right to give this also?" The police officer, unable to answer Chapman's question, allowed him to continue with his mission.

He had a fire that could not be quenched.

A HOUSE FOR EVERYONE

Another vital ministry was through Chapman's home. Not long after accepting the pastorate at Ebenezer Strict Baptist Chapel, he purchased a large house in a dilapidated district. Not too many wanted to reside in this neighborhood. The streets were filthy and a tannery was nearby that emitted vile odors. When Captain Henry Chapman, an inquisitive relative, visited, he was shocked by what he discovered. When dropped off at the residence, Henry assured the cab driver that there must have been a mistake. He said, "This could not possibly be the home of Robert Chapman!"

Chapman wanted to make his home to be a hospitable place for Christian workers and evangelists. Since he remained a bachelor all his life, he didn't have to worry about what a wife would think if people stayed over. Chapman welcomed many to come and stay with him for free.

Several evangelists from abroad lodged with him while

preaching in London. Whether they stayed a day or for weeks made no difference to Chapman. His door was always open. Chapman was heard saying on more than one occasion, "Dear brother, if you came by invitation, you are welcome; if you came without invitation, you are doubly welcome."

Many visitors to Chapman's house were astonished when, after they arrived, they were shown to their bedroom, told what the habits of the household were, and encouraged to leave their boots outside the bedroom door for Mr. Chapman to clean and shine. Chapman took it upon himself to daily polish the boots and shoes of his guests and when they protested he said, "Jesus taught us to wash the saints feet; that in modern civilization the nearest approach to obedience to that command was to black their boots."

Chapman never worried about running out of food or having enough room. He said, "The Lord takes care of that," and for over seventy years, all his needs were supplied. From week to week, he did not know how the pantry would be stocked or where the wood for the fireplace would come from. There was no way in the natural all his everyday essentials could be covered, but God always provided for him.

Sometimes, at the end of the day, money would run out or there would be no provisions left in the house. But this was not an emergency to Chapman. He would "just pray about it." Invariably, by the next morning, breakfast would always be provided for. His guests never sensed that anything was amiss. Chapman gave them no indication that there was any need.

Chapman truly trusted in God for everything and he wanted to teach others the same principle. So, he never wanted to convey that the dependency on God was an extraordinary thing. He was convinced that it should be the natural life-style for a Christian.

Once, when Chapman's cousin visited, he was curious about how such a large household was supplied with such meager means. When he looked into the pantry, he saw that the shelves were almost bare. This relative told Chapman that he wanted to purchase groceries and rectify his problem. Chapman agreed, under one condition. The groceries could only be bought at a particular shop. The cousin accepted this condition. One of Chapman's biographers recounts the rest of this compelling story:

> "When the grocer asked where the goods were to be sent, and was directed to send them to Robert Chapman, his face changed, and he said he feared the order had been placed at the wrong shop. 'No... my cousin... specially directed me to come to you.' A tear came on the grocer's cheek: 'I have heard of such things being done, but I never thought they really were. It was only last Saturday, at an open-air meeting, that I spat on Mr. Chapman's face.' The man was completely broken down by this because he had for years made Mr. Chapman the target of his abuse and wicked criticism."

It wasn't long before this grocer was on his face before Chapman, laying in a posture of sincere repentance. He pleaded for forgiveness and gave his life to Jesus. This was truly a marvelous display of forgiveness and grace. Even in dealing with enemies, Chapman demonstrated patience. The intercessor always displayed brotherly love to all.

PRAYER AND INTERCESSION

Unsurprisingly, prayer and intercession were a prominent part of Chapman's life. It gave him the means of establishing an intimate relationship with the Father. Chapman once said, "When I bow to God, God stoops to me. As the father and child do all they can to please each other, so I do all I can to please God, and God does all He can to please me."

Chapman would pray daily for his congregation, city, guests, family, friends, and all the eternal interests of the kingdom of God. He believed that a servant of God should spend as much time in prayer and the word of God as other men do at their workbenches.

On weekdays, Chapman woke up at 4:00 am and spent the first seven hours of the day in spiritual communion with God. While he read scripture, biblically-soaked prayers came forth from his mouth. Chapman said, "It is one thing to read the bible, choosing something that suits me (as is shamefully said), and another thing to search it that I may become acquainted with God in Christ."

On Saturdays, Chapman changed his routine without compromising his prayer life. He spent most of the day in his carpentry workshop in the corner of his home. This enabled the intersection of the spiritual and the practical. While working with wood, Chapman fasted and poured out his soul in prayer. He sincerely believed that there was no distinction between spiritual or natural duties, "And whatever you do, do it heartily, as to the Lord and not to men." (Colossians 3:23)

The famous missionary to China, Hudson Taylor, spent a Saturday or two with Chapman and later shared the following reflection:

"Saturday was the day Mr. Robert Chapman set apart for special waiting upon God, though it was his habit to arise always at or before daylight and give hours to fervent intercession . . . His workshop claimed him, however, in a special way at the close of the week. It was his sanctum, containing little but his turning lathe and a shelf on which he could lay his bible. Here he spent hours at a time, denying himself . . . to any and every visitor, and going without his midday meal that he might be the freer in spirit. The mechanical occupation of the lathe he found helpful to a connected line of thought; so looking at the bible from time to time, or dropping to his knees in prayer, he would turn out plates . . . his mind occupied . . . with the eternal interests of the kingdom of God."

Chapman spent hours in prayer and discovered how to petition the throne room of heaven. Occasionally he shared some insights that came through his times of intercession. On one occasion, he recounted the following:

"One of the best answers to prayer is to be able to continue in prayer . . . Our need of prayer is as frequent as the moments of the day; and as we grow in spiritual mind, our continual needs will be felt by us more and more."

While Hudson Taylor was laboring as a missionary in China, Chapman "labored" alongside of him in prayer, daily. When Hudson returned, after seven years on the mission field, he mentioned that it was good to see his friend after so long a time. Chapman said, "Dear brother, I have visited you every day since you went to China."

A man who knew Chapman and visited some of his services also wanted to share some of what this great intercessor comprehended. He shared the following:

"It was laid on his heart... that the world stood in great need of intercession, and that intercession was to be particularly his vocation; therefore his first and best hours are given to prayer... He preaches to 800 souls every Sunday; he undertakes pastoral work; he attends to the minutest bodily and spiritual wants of a stream of visitors, some of whom stay for an hour, some for a month... it was his practice to... take away the boots of his guests, to clean them with his own hands."

The great revivalist, Leonard Ravenhill, once declared, "No

man is greater than his prayer life." Robert Cleaver Chapman undoubtedly understood this. This was the secret of his inexplicable joy and his spiritual power.

A GIANT IN THE LAND

Chapman's devotion and unending intercession affected multitudes. Amazingly, Chapman preached his last sermon on his ninety-eighth birthday. His fervent prayers were only silenced after he uttered his dying breath. The last words on Chapman's lips were, "The peace of God, which passes all understanding."

Robert Cleaver Chapman was a powerful man of God who taught many the meaning of prayer. Speaking of him, J. R. Caldwell said, "Truly the memory of his visit remains with us as a precious illustration of how far God can reproduce in a believer, even here, the image of His Son." A. T. Pierson, an author and celebrated orator said that Chapman brought to mind the biblical words, "There were giants on the earth in those days."

"It is no longer I who live, but Christ lives in me" (Galatians 2:20).

8

THE GREAT PRAYER REVIVAL 1857-1858 (PART ONE)

Jeremiah Lanphier

"Prayer is a catalyst for revival as gasoline is to fire." —Frank Di Pietro

"We shall never see much change for the better in our churches in general till the prayer meeting occupies a high place in the esteem of Christians." —Charles Spurgeon

"If revival in the land depended on your prayers, your faith, or your obedience, would we ever experience revival?" —Del Fehsenfeld Jr.

"The effective, fervent prayer of a righteous man avails much." —James, the Apostle (James 5:16).

"There is such a general confidence in the prevalence of prayer that the people very extensively seemed to prefer meeting for prayer to meeting for preaching. The general impression seemed to be, 'We have had instruction until we are hardened; it is time for us to pray.—Charles Finney

R evivals can break open unexpectedly. Multitudes of people can intercede at once. As the March 20, 1858 edition of the *New York Times* hit the street, it broke news on a powerful move of God. The editorial declared:

"The great wave of religious excitement which is now sweeping over this nation, is one of the most remarkable movements since the reformation… Travelers relate that in cars and steamboats, in banks and markets, everywhere through the interior, this matter is an absorbing topic. Churches are crowded; bank-directors rooms become oratories; school houses are turned into chapels; converts are numbered by the scores of thousands. In this city, we have beheld a sight which not the most enthusiastic fanatic from church-observances could ever have hoped to look upon; we have seen in a business-quarter of the City, in the busiest hours, assemblies of merchants, clerks and working men, to the number of five thousand, gathered day after day for a simple and solemn worship. Similar assemblies we find in other portions of the City; a theatre is turned into a chapel; churches of all sects are open and crowded by day and night... It is most impressive to think that over this great land tens and fifties of thousands of men and women are putting themselves at this time in a simple, serious way, the greatest question that can ever come before the human mind 'What shall I do to be saved?'"

Shortly, spiritual hunger would be on display across the United States. People read not only reports from New York. Newspapers in Chicago, San Francisco, Boston, and smaller cities across the heartland had similar accounts. God was doing a new work in America.

As the people began praying, they were turned upside down. A startling wave of repentance affected judges, politicians, businessmen, housewives, and students. Both Christians and sin-soaked non-believers were being touched by the hand of God.

Schools closed to give people an opportunity to pray and seek God. The fact that most cities, colleges, and institutions were simultaneously impacted is staggering to the imagination.

Not long after the New York Times article, over 10,000 Wall Street businessmen gathered in prayer. But this wasn't a one time event. These men and countless others began interceding daily in a public forum.

By May 1858, mere months after a burden of prayer fell on the city, New York churches experienced exponential growth. Over 50,000 new converts were added to membership rolls.

Within one year, over one million new converts were recorded and many already attending church claimed that they were truly born again.

The reports of life-change were astounding. One traveler, attending a prayer meeting in Boston, declared,

"I am from Omaha, the capitol of Nebraska. On my journey east,
I have found a continuous prayer meeting all the way. We call it
about two thousand miles from Omaha to Boston; and here was
a prayer meeting about two thousand miles in extent."

What was transpiring in America, and soon the world, was
the work of the sovereign Hand of God. This revival featured no
particular evangelist, church, or organizational matrix. It was
completely non-sectarian—welcoming participation from every
Bible-believing Christian.

Divisive doctrines were sidelined, and instead, concerns
about the condition of souls captured the gaze of the masses.
The Spirit of God shook the country on a mass level—without
the dictates of man. It was revival God's way! This wonderful
outpouring of intercessory prayer and repentance is one of the
greatest moves of God in history.

Some participants called this movement "The Laymen's
Revival" because it was carried forward by non-clergy
intercession and activism. Others preferred to title it, "The
Prayer Meeting Revival." The actual name is less important than
what it instituted. This powerful intercessory movement
exploded into the Third Great Awakening.

DYING EMBERS

Over the centuries, God's Spirit was repeatedly poured out on
America through revivals and awakenings. Sadly, around a
generation after a soul-shaking move of God, the spiritual fervor
waned. What was once a raging fire became a dying ember. Like
the common biblical pattern of apostasy, new generations turned
from the faith of their fathers. "Israel served the Lord all the days
of Joshua and all the days of the elders who outlived Joshua, and
had known all the works of the Lord which He had done for
Israel" (Joshua 24:31 AMP).

By the mid-1800s, many of the great revivalists of old had passed on, and religious life in America was in decline. Once fervent congregations were losing half of their families as worldliness and lethargy gripped the nation. This was an era of prosperity and growth, and many turned their attention toward the acquisition of wealth. They were more interested in money than God. "Americanism," a hypnotic materialism and belief in utopia, had gripped the nation, and the people needed to be shocked out of their stupor.

God has a way of disrupting our well-ordered worlds, particularly when they are built without Him in mind. This ungodly stronghold in America was abruptly broken in the "Bank Panic of October 1857." In October, the United States' banks and financial systems collapsed, causing a severe financial panic. It brought tens of thousands of people to ruin in the industrial centers of the nation.

The American economy was decimated as businesses collapsed. Multi-millionaires lost their fortunes as the stock market crashed. In addition, it forced railroads into bankruptcy, slowing down the ability to transport goods. People were astounded as eighteen New York banks suspended operations and refused to honor promissory notes. To make matters worse, the largest U.S. corporation, the Ohio Life Insurance and Trust Company, failed, and along with that, thousands of jobs disappeared.

As hopelessness arose, other problems came to a head. People lost their homes and were forced to roam the streets. Thousands were trying to figure out where to get their next meal. Amid this disruption, violence intensified. Spousal abuse and murder increased throughout the industrial centers. Tragically, suicide also became common. At one point, the number of people taking their own lives doubled in one day.

This was a trying time. Although the people didn't know it,

the Civil War was just over the horizon. The United States of America tottered on the brink of disaster.

It's understood that wrong pursuits motivate unbelievers. Why would the ungodly obey the Bible? They know nothing of its teachings. But Christians are supposed to be different. We don't get caught up in the things that entertain the masses. We have a much higher purpose.

Nevertheless, in the mid-1800s, many Christians became entangled in the lust, the flesh, and the pride of life. Some believed God was disrupting the financial systems to regain the attention of his bride. Be assured that God will not compete with anything—including wealth and possessions. He alone is Lord!

Leading up to this crisis, God was revealing the problems to the intercessors. Under the unction of the Holy Spirit, they were distressed about the selfishness and materialism infesting believers. They prayed God would sovereignly intervene and bring a revival to the nation. The Lord was already answering their prayers.

THE RUMBLINGS OF REVIVAL

The earliest tremors of a North American revival were evidenced in a gathering of Presbyterian leaders. Declaring the necessity of fasting, humility, and prayer, they organized a three-day convention in December 1856. Coming out of this gathering, they published some of the messages, and an appeal for corporate prayer, in a book titled, "Longing for Revivals." In its pages, they declared, "We trust that the period is not distant, when this state of actual general revival shall be ours." These words stirred the hearts of many.

Baptist and Methodist pastors were also crying out to God to send another awakening to America. One intercessor wrote, come oh Lord, so "that the popular addiction of money-making might be broken."

Lots of intercession was beginning to take place. In the summer of 1857, Walter and Phoebe Palmer, a Methodist physician, and his wife started prayer meetings in Hamilton, Canada. This gathering turned into a glorious revival. One newspaper reporter note,

> "persons of all classes... men of low degree and high estate for wealth and position, old and maidens, and even little children... can be seen kneeling together... even the mayor of the city along with other persons of like position... are not ashamed to be seen bowed at the altar of prayer beside the humblest person."

At this time, a revival also broke open in Charlestown, South Carolina among enslaved African-Americans. The Anson Street Presbyterian Church had sixty members—forty-eight of which were slaves. The congregation gathered every night for eight weeks and services lasted until midnight. Crowds of as many as two thousand pressed to get into these powerful revival meetings. Hundreds were converted and became faithful members of various churches across the city.

Although trouble was on the horizon, there were pockets of revival being reported in various parts of the United States. These events would be the kindling that would help ignite a national awakening in the months ahead. The power of darkness was about to bow its knee.

JEREMIAH LANPHIER

The North Dutch Reformed Church, on the corner of Fulton and William Streets in Manhattan, New York, knew things needed to change if they wanted to stay viable. Like many other congregations in the mid-1800s, they had a noticeable decline in membership. The board knew they needed to refocus on evangelism.

On July 1, 1857, the leaders appointed 48-year-old Jeremiah Lanphier to be their "street missionary." He was a tall, quiet man "with a pleasant face, and affectionate manner... shrewd and endowed with much tact and common sense." Lanphier was converted fifteen years earlier at Charles Finney's Broadway Tabernacle and never lost his zeal.

Being a merchant, Lanphier had no experience in evangelism. Nevertheless, he gladly gave up his trade position to knock on doors for less than $1,000 a year. As he started to work, he saw little fruit in his efforts. Day after day, after returning home weary and discouraged, he took his frustration to the Lord in prayer.

Lanphier genuinely cared for the people, and God put the burden of intercession on him. He spent hours seeking the face of God for the salvation of Manhattan. Amid his intercessory efforts, he was led to start a weekly prayer meeting for business people. He knew businesses shut down at noon every day for lunch. So, he thought some might take advantage of this time to pray. Lanphier created a small advertisement, promoting the fact that the church was open for prayer.

DAILY
PRAYER MEETING
From 12 to 1 o'clock.

— STOP —
5, 10, or 20 Minutes,
or the whole hour,
AS YOUR TIME ADMITS.

Lanphier walked the neighborhoods near the church and left the handbill in all the offices and warehouses that he could visit. While he walked on the streets, he would stop businessmen and let them know about the prayer meeting. Lanphier made up other print materials that he passed out. One of which was a pamphlet titled, "How Often Should I Pray." Over time, he gave out thousands of notices about the intercessory gathering.

The date for the first businessmen's prayer meeting at Lanphier's church was set for September 23, 1857. As he was preparing things for the people to arrive, he placed a poster at the church entrance, title, "Rules for the Prayer Meeting."

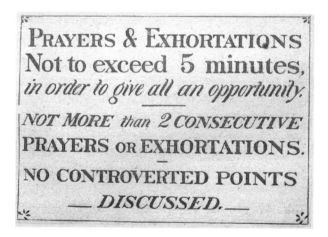

Ten minutes before noon on Wednesday, the day chosen for the prayer meeting, Lanphier unlocked the doors and climbed to the third floor. As the sound of the creaking stairs echoed through the empty church, he entered the empty room and waited. The population of New York, at that time, was over a million people. Maybe hundreds or thousands would show up? But when the clock struck noon, only one person showed for prayer, Lanphier himself.

The evangelist was disappointed but undeterred. He knelt

and stormed the throne of grace—not wasting a moment of time. Ten minutes passed and then ten minutes more. Finally, at 12:30, he heard footsteps on the stairs. One man entered into the room and then another. Before long, there was six. They spent the remainder of the hour in heartfelt prayer.

As the gathering ended, Lanphier suggested that they meet together again the next week, and the participants agreed. That was it. Nothing extraordinary happened. There was no earth-shaking outpouring of the Spirit. No one, including Lanphier, had any inkling that the meeting was the beginning of one of the greatest awakenings to sweep the nation—bringing one million souls into the Kingdom of God.

URGENCY OF INTERCESSSION

As Lanphier interceded, revival was far from his mind. He was burdened by the urgency of intercession. His only concern was that the families in Manhattan should learn to pray and seek the Lord, starting with the father. He did not know that his efforts would help spark a national awakening.

Lanphier wasn't a fiery evangelist like Charles Finney. He wasn't a high level church official, and he had no airs about him. Lanphier merely sought God. He was humble enough to go low and do what was needed to fulfill God's purposes. Like Esther, Lanphier was called "for a time such as this."

Because of what was stirring in his heart, Lanphier knew that seeking the Lord was foundational. He understood, like the great revivalist John Wesley, "God does nothing but in answer to prayer." History is forever changed when the saints intercede.

The evangelist, humbly bowing to the Sovereignty of the Lord of Hosts, led the way into fervent intercession. Soon millions would follow. Through Lanphier, God would restore His glory to the American church on the eve of the Civil War. As these powerful prayers arose, God split the heavens and awakened a sleeping church.

> "If My people who are called by My name will humble themselves, and pray and seek My face, and turn from their wicked ways, then I will hear from heaven, and will forgive their sin and heal their land" (2 Chronicles 7:14).

9

THE GREAT PRAYER REVIVAL 1857-1858 (PART TWO)

Noon Time Prayer Meeting

"If we can have a worldwide pandemic, we can have a worldwide revival."—Steve Gray

"All the true revivals have been born of prayer. When God's people become so concerned with the state of religion that they lay on their faces day and night in earnest supplication, the blessing will be sure to fall."—E. M. Bounds

"Work as if you were to live a hundred years; pray as if you were to die tomorrow."—Benjamin Franklin

"We should seek not too much to pray but to become prayer."—St. Francis of Assisi

"Today, many leaders are so consumed with doing 'busy church' work they cannot hear God directing them into 'Kingdom work.' We need to get control of the many 'Martha's in our ministries and slow down to spend time with the 'Mary.'"—Frank Di Pietro

When revival erupts, it changes everything. This was certainly what occurred during the Great Prayer Revival that opened the door to the Third Great Awakening.

The Washington National Intelligencer reported, during this revival, several New England towns did not have a single unconverted person within their city limits. Sweeping moves of the Spirit were being recorded in state after state.

Across America, in hamlets, small towns, and major metro areas, church bells sounded daily, summoning people to pray. Charles Grandison Finney, one of America's most prominent evangelists, wrote about what was occurring:

"This was in the winter of 1857-58; and it will be remembered that it was at this time that a great revival prevailed throughout the land in such a tremendous manner, that for some weeks it was estimated that not less than fifty thousand conversions occurred per week."

God was waking the spiritually dead and the apathetic members of His church. Today historians barely reference the Great Prayer Revival of 1857-1858, but in the annals of the Kingdom, it will be one of the greatest American awakenings.

John Wesley once told his followers, "Bear up the hands that hang down, by faith and prayer... Storm the throne of Grace and persevere therein and mercy will come down." This is what these watchmen did. Beginning September 23, 1857, Jeremiah Lanphier and six other intercessors stood on the wall and would not keep silent until God came to bless His Church (Isaiah 62:6). God heard their cries and answered. The fire fell.

After that historic first prayer meeting, Lanphier and those attending agreed to meet again on Wednesday, September 30th. Before the men departed, Lanphier recounted the following message:

> "How Often Shall I Pray? As often as the language of prayer is in my heart; as often as I see my need of help; as often as I feel the power of temptation; as often as I am made sensible of any spiritual declension, or feel the aggression of a worldly, earthly spirit... In prayer, we leave the business of time for that of eternity, and intercourse with God."

At the next prayer meeting, twenty men showed up. Momentum began building. On the following Wednesday— October 7—forty stood on the prayer floor. Lanphier was encouraged and recommended that they make the prayer meeting a daily occurrence. Everyone agreed that this was sensible.

Over subsequent days, the prayer meeting surpassed 100 participants, and it kept increasing. On Wednesday, October 14, news broke about a horrible financial panic. This outcome was devastating to the whole nation, but particularly unsettling for the inhabitants of Manhattan.

Unsurprisingly, the "Fulton Street Prayer Meeting," as it was named, swelled even more with those concerned about their livelihoods. The Old Dutch Church overflowed with over three thousand interceding daily.

In the beginning, it was primarily businessmen. But with time, people from every walk of life came through the doors. One would find bankers, brokers, lawyers, physicians, manufacturers, merchants, mechanics, clerks, and messenger boys. Often, taxi drivers and cargo haulers parked their wagons and came in for a few minutes of prayer before continuing their routes. God was uniting people from all walks of life in prayer.

By November, Lanphier began holding three meetings simultaneously in various rooms in the church. So many attended that it forced them to move the intercessory gatherings to local theaters and opera houses. A powerful move of God was underway.

Within six months, the noon-time prayer meetings in New York were attracting tens of thousands of people. The New York Times, The New York Herald, and the New York Tribune dedicated entire issues to the revival. Reporters swarmed the meetings. As the awakening's growth and impact were explored in print, "The Progress of the Revival" became a common headline.

One story recounted the change that occurred in the life of a well-known criminal and prize fighter called, "Awful Gardenier." When he came to the prayer meeting, he gave his life to Christ. Gardenier visited Sing Sing Penitentiary and gave his testimony to the convicts. Many responded to the message, including the noted river thief, Jerry McAuley, who would later establish the Water Street Mission.

Many Americans, concerned about the nation's economic

woes, were captivated by the stories of the prayer meetings taking place in New York. Christian leaders in other cities organized their own prayer meetings, which produced similar outcomes.

Business leaders organized a prayer meeting in Philadelphia. The largest facility in the city, Jayne's Hall, was obtained, and soon overflowing with intercessors. Wesley Duewel recounts that, "Meetings were held at noon each day in public halls, concert halls, fire stations, houses and tents. The whole city exuded a spirit of prayer."

The incense of prayer also rose in Boston, Baltimore, Washington, D.C., Richmond, Charleston, Savannah, Birmingham, Mobile, New Orleans, Vicksburg, Memphis, St. Louis, Kansas City, Pittsburgh, Cincinnati, and Chicago. Fervent intercession was taking place everywhere in the U.S.

On the doors of businesses hung the sign, "Closed, will reopen at the close of the prayer meeting." They held five meetings a day in Washington, D.C. with five thousand attending each gathering. In Philadelphia, six thousand attended the daily meetings. A Spiritual contentment ruled the day. The services comprised "simple prayer, exhortation and singing… so earnest, so solemn, the silence… so awful, the singing… so over-powering." Those attending would never forget the feeling of awe and wonderment of His beauty, splendor, and majesty.

NEWSPAPER HEADLINES

In every city, newspaper reporters followed the pattern of journalists in New York. They wrote about impassioned prayer of the Christians. Major stories about prayer meetings in San Francisco, Chicago, and Cincinnati took over the front page of the papers. Things even stirred in parts of Canada.

In 1858, across the United States, bold banner headlines affirmed the goodness of God:

NEW HAVEN, CONNECTICUT—CITY'S BIGGEST CHURCH
PACKED TWICE DAILY FOR PRAYER

BETHEL, CONNECTICUT—BUSINESSES SHUT DOWN FOR
HOUR EACH DAY; EVERYBODY PRAYS.

ALBANY, NEW YORK—STATE LEGISLATORS GET DOWN
ON KNEES

SCHENECTADY, NEW YORK—ICE ON THE MOHAWK
BROKEN FOR BAPTISMS

NEWARK, NEW YORK—FIREMEN'S PRAYER MEETING
ATTRACTS 2000

WASHINGTON, D.C.—FIVE PRAYER MEETINGS GO
AROUND THE CLOCK

NEW HAVEN, CONNECTICUT—REVIVAL SWEEPS YALE
UNIVERSITY

HARVEST OF SOULS

There was an awesome sense of God's presence hovering over
the United States. Testimonies and eyewitness reports affirmed
that prayers were being answered and people were experiencing
the goodness and wonder of the gospel. Faith was at an all-time
high.

People from every walk of life, from judges to mechanics,
were all bowing down in prayer before the altar of Almighty God.
In several cities, opera halls and other larger venues opened their
doors to handle the influx of those wanting to pray. When
buildings weren't available, they would gather in factories,
stores, and open parks. If necessary, some even prayed in the

muddy city streets. At this time, thousands came together with neighbors to pray around the dinner table.

Ministers did not lead the revival; it was carried forward by anointed laypeople. Also, it was not confined to only one denomination. Although the fire began in a Dutch Reformed Church, the sparks also ignited in Baptist, Methodist, and Episcopalian congregations. People who once argued about doctrine were now praying together.

Although pastors were not leading it, they wanted to do their part to pull in the harvest of souls. Hundreds of church leaders began holding morning, afternoon, and evening prayer meetings for those concerned about their souls. They were eager to counsel the repentant.

Mass conversions were now common as hundreds of city dwellers gave their hearts to God, hourly. At one point, fifty-thousand sinners committed their lives to Jesus, weekly, across the United States. Tens of thousands of converts were joining Churches each week. In one year, over one million names were added to the "Lamb's book of life."

God was doing so many wonderful things. At this time, sin was scarce because the houses of ill-repute, the gambling halls, the race tracks, the taverns—places of debauchery—were closed up.

REVIVAL ON THE SEA

For many, the revival in 1858 felt like a spiritual typhoon overtaking the earth. Foreign ships, hundreds of miles from American harbors, felt the solemn presence of the Holy Spirit. Reports indicate that revival broke out on the vessels as passengers felt the weight of their sins.

Navigational logs provide shocking evidence of the helmsmasters' communications. As one ship neared the harbor, the captain franticly wrote, "Have ministers available." When another boat docked, they discovered that every individual on board, including the crew, was converted one hundred and fifty miles from shore.

There are many similar stories. One of the more compelling accounts of revival moving on the sea occurred in the New York harbor. They anchored the battleship North Carolina, with more than a thousand men aboard, and then God moved. Four sailors knelt to pray on the lower deck. As they interceded, the Holy Spirit filled their hearts and broke out in praise. Wesley Duewel finishes the story,

> "Ungodly men on the top deck heard the singing, looked down, and saw the boys kneeling. They began running down the stairs, mocking and jeering… by the time they reached the bottom deck they fell on their knees and began crying for mercy."

A few sparks became a burning flame. As ungodly sailors turned to the Lord, others followed after them. Soon virtually the entire ship was converted. They brought ministers in to help men travailing over their souls. This fervor spread to the crew on other ships. The North Carolina, a massive vessel of war, became an unexpected center of revival.

NOT GRIEVING THE SPIRIT

A burning desire for more of the things of God and intense prayer flamed in the heart of America. Heavenly talk was on the lips of almost everyone. Religion was the common topic of conversation. People discussed various topics, but invariably Kingdom principles were foremost.

An underlying rule in the prayer rooms was not to grieve the Holy Spirit. What grieved God grieved the people. The intercessory gatherings were God-appointed, God-presided, and God-enlightened. From the lowest pauper to the highest office seekers, prayer was the fire that ignited the soul. Abraham Lincoln, on the eve of presidential ambitions, declared, "I have been driven many times upon my knees by the overwhelming conviction that I had nowhere else to go."

As the glory of God covered the country, the "Third Great Awakening" was breathing life into a dying nation.

REVIVAL IN THE CIVIL WAR

With the entrance of the bloody Civil War, many believed the Awakening would wane. But this was not the case. Although newspapers turned their attention to this terrible, divisive scourge, many believers still focused on intercession. Only God could unify a divided nation. The fervor of revival in their hearts continued to burn.

In the autumn of 1861—in a Richmond, Virginia, military hospital—a renewed spirit of intercession gripped the hearts of wounded soldiers. Many of these men still carried the flame from 1857 to 1858. They knew what it meant to seek the face of God. In time, the fervor would spread to the armies on both sides of the conflict.

It surprises some to learn that generals in the Southern armies, like Robert E. Lee and Thomas J. "Stonewall" Jackson, labored to fan the flames of revival in the troops. They not only encouraged their men to pray, they actively participated in the times of worship. God is no respecter of persons.

During the winter of 1863, a revival erupted in the First Brigade, Second Corps of the Army of Northern Virginia. This impassioned group was known as the "Stonewall Brigade." This stirring began with a series of prayer meetings led by soldiers. In this overflow of the Prayer Meetings of 1857-1858, ministers were not leading; it was the Spirit of God. What later became known as "The Great Confederate Revival of 1863" compelled 150,000 men in Lee's army to turn to Christ.

This fervent revival spread from the Army of Northern Virginia to the Army of the Tennessee. In Chattanooga, it jumped the Confederate lines and crossed over into the Union Army.

In the Chickamauga Creek, near Ringgold, Georgia, they baptized thousands of Union soldiers. As these marvelous declarations of faith transpired, Confederate soldiers watched from a mountaintop nearby. Surprisingly, they roared as they witnessed their opponents' public affirmation of Jesus.

The revival in the armies continued until the end of the war, sweeping 150,000 to 200,000 men on each side into the Kingdom.

BROKEN PRAYER

Although there was substantial pain, God was powerfully at work during the nineteenth century. Even the far-reaching tragedies of economic collapse and the Civil War could not hold back the spirit of intercession. Many men and women—the just and the unjust—discovered what it meant to seek the Lord. More importantly, the once despondent church was reinvigorated and operating in unspeakable glory.

American Christians, though broken in battle, became consumed with intimacy with God. Long after people talked about what transpired on Fulton Street in 1857, a similar temperament prevailed. Out of humble hearts, the sound of broken prayer ascended to heaven.

"Then you will call upon Me and go and pray to Me, and I will listen to you. And you will seek Me and find Me, when you search for Me with all your heart." — Jeremiah 29:12-13

10

THE ULSTER REVIVAL OF 1859

James McQuilkin

"Neglect of prayer is the main obstacle to holiness."—John
Wesley

"Evangelism is where man makes the altar call. Revival is where
God makes the altar call."—Leonard Ravenhill

"A revived Church is the only hope for a dying world."—Andrew
Murray

"I will have success! I will wear the knees of my pants out and
tear a hole through heaven. God must come to me!"—J.H.
Weber

"To your knees, man! And to your Bible! Decide at once! Do not
hedge! Time flies! Cease your insults to God. Quit consulting
flesh and blood. Stop your lame lying and excuses. You sought in
time past for Jesus to be king over you. NOW then DO IT!" —
C.T. Studd

Revival erupted in the United States in 1857, but God had
His sights on something much bigger—Europe. The
Anglican Church, like most mid-nineteenth century
congregations in America, was in a stupor. They were dying a
slow death.

A yearning for awakening was prevalent, and hearing of the
"Pentecost" that fell on America, hope stirred. Reports came
from across the Atlantic of the thousands converted in the
numerous American prayer meetings.

Newspaper reports and eyewitness testimonies of what was
taking place in the United States stirred a "Holy Desperation" in
the hearts of the Irish people. Presbyterians in Northern Ireland,
hearing of the fervor, sent a delegation to Philadelphia to see "if
such things were really true." Returning home, the men reported
the strange and holy events taking place. The embers in their
hearts were stirred, and a flame arose. One delegate proclaimed,

"I rejoice in the decided conviction that it (revival/awakening) is
the 'Lord's doing;' unaccountable by any natural causes, entirely

above and beyond what any human device or power could produce; an outpouring of the Spirit of God upon God's people, quickening them to greater earnestness in His service; and upon the unconverted, to make them new creatures in Christ Jesus."

It wasn't long before things stirred in other parts of Europe. The Prayer Revival of 1857-58 jumped the Atlantic Ocean. Like a tidal wave, the glory of God overtook Ireland, Scotland, England, and South Africa. Soon, the waters of restoration had risen in the four corners of the earth.

This fresh wave of revival had many of the same characteristics as were witnessed in the United States—it was foremost a prayer awakening. In its glorious fervor, it brought thousands into the Kingdom.

Churchgoers in the mid-nineteenth century were only nominally Christian. Many Europeans attended Sunday services but were lethargic. This backslidden condition was particularly evident in the nine counties of Northern Ireland called "Ulster." Many church workers were discouraged by the religious complacency and the "fruitless ministries." One wrote,

"Hitherto, our condition was deplorable. The congregation seemed dead to God... They are formal, cold, prayerless, worldly, and stingy in religious things. Twice I tried a prayer meeting of my elders, but failed; for after the fifth or sixth night, I was alone. Year after year passed; yet still no fruit. What alarmed me most was the indisposition, almost hostility of the people to meetings of prayer... that I was unnecessarily disturbing them. I had never been so desponding or distressed as during the weeks immediately preceding the awakening. I had almost ceased to hope... and I told my people... I was appalled... and that we would... be left utterly reprobate."

He wasn't the only leader witnessing the breakdown. Another

wrote, "There seemed great coldness and deadness. I had preached the Gospel faithfully, earnestly, and plainly for eleven years; yet it was not known to me that a single individual had been converted." Sounding a similar alarm, a concerned pastor declared, "The congregation was in a most unsatisfactory state; in fact altogether Laodicean."

Although Ulster intercessors had been praying for years, they witnessed no change in the spiritual condition of their land. It felt like a hopeless situation. But they knew God was greater than their circumstances. Though it was dark, they didn't want to let up. They remembered the words of Jesus: "With men this is impossible, but with God all things are possible" (Matthew 19:26). Prayers went up and the power of God came down. The course of Christendom was altered.

THE LAST PLEAS OF MRS. COLVILLE

In Kells, Ireland, some devout men were enthused. They were concerned about the condition of the church, but grew hopeful about the works of God. The intercessors started a prayer meeting asking the Lord to bring a revival to their nation. They knew it would be a long row to hoe. Although the ground was "fallow," they were heartened, knowing the seeds of prayer were being planted.

The men prayed and waited. They fervently interceded, expecting the covenant-keeping God to stand by His word. He did, but in His own perfect timing.

When God brings awakening, He searches for the right kindling. The Lord wants to have someone who can carry the fire before He lights the flame. Those God ignites often come from unlikely corners of the church.

Great things can come from unexpected sources. A missionary from the Baptist Missionary Society of England, known only as Mrs. Colville, visited Ballymena, Ireland, in the spring of 1856. She went door to door, spreading the good news of Jesus. Many did not like what she had to say and they slammed the door in her face. Four months later, Colville planned to return to England. Broken and discouraged, she was not only angry about her fruitlessness, she wondered why God did not seem to favor her labors.

Just days before leaving Ireland, Colville visited a young woman dying in her home. After coming through the door, she encountered other members of the family. The entire household, including the sickly woman, was apathetic in their faith. The missionary prayed for the diseased woman and then spoke to the others about true devotion to Christ.

The family and guests listened to Colville, but weren't enthused by her remarks. A young man tersely asked, "Are you a Calvinist?" Not wanting to be drawn into a denominational debate, she answered, "I would not wish to be more or less a Calvinist than our Lord and His apostles. But, I do not care to talk on mere points of doctrine. I would rather speak of the experience of salvation in the soul. If one were to tell me what he knows of the state of his heart towards God, I think I could tell him whether he knows the Lord Jesus savingly."

There was no outward sign of conviction, but Colville continued to stir the hearts of her listeners. She shifted the discussion to Matthew 7:21-23: "I never knew you; depart from Me." She didn't know it, but the words of scripture had cut through this young man's hard religious exterior. These truths were like an arrow piercing his conscience. Colville left, not knowing that she planted a seed in the heart of the young man that, within a year and a half, would grow into a move of God that would sweep multitudes into the Kingdom. Little did she know that she had finally found her purpose for coming to Ireland.

JAMES MCQUILKIN

The young man Colville ministered to that day was James McQuilkin. He had traveled five miles from his home in Kells to visit the dying women and her friends. He had much to say about religion to this missionary, but his words were empty and dry.

McQuikin was a backslidden Presbyterian who dabbled in worldly pursuits more than scriptural readings and prayer. Although McQuikin was a linen manufacturer, what he enjoyed was raising "fighting cocks." This shady sideline business was profitable because of the gambling atmosphere that prevailed in Ireland. He was on the wrong road, but Jesus was about to intervene.

After McQuilkin's meeting with Colville, he experienced a soul-wrenching sense of conviction. After considerable time in prayer, he found peace. Jesus brought forgiveness and salvation. News spread that McQuikin, known as a sinful man, surrendered to Jesus Christ.

This young convert organized a prayer meeting in September 1857, inviting many of his friends and family. Coincidently, this was the same week Jeremiah Lanphier, at the Old Dutch Church on Fulton Street, New York City launched his work. It is true when the Bible declares, "God rules and reigns over the affairs of men" (Daniel 4:17).

McQuilkin and the Irishmen began their prayer meeting in an old schoolhouse in Kells. As they interceded, they believed God was about to do something wonderful in Ireland. They were hopeful, but did not know what was going to take place.

As these men continued to meet and pray, reports of the awakening in the United States came to their attention. Over the months, Irish newspapers increasingly reported on the strange, spiritual phenomenon overseas.

Awe and wonder swept through this small country. They sent ambassadors across the Atlantic to bring back a first-hand report.

Dr. William Gibson and Rev. William McClure traveled to New York to visit the Fulton Street prayer meeting and see if it was of God. When the men returned to Ireland, they reported on this unprecedented awakening. They assured their colleagues that the newspapers didn't report half of what God was doing.

Gibson and McClure declared that intercession was the driving force of the revival—but not just any entreaty before God. This awakening was carried on the back of prevailing prayer. The deeper the prayers, the deeper that God moved.

Those who heard Gibson and McClure's report were awestruck. A "righteous jealousy" and "holy desperation" came over them. They longed to have the same kinds of intercessory experiences in their homeland.

By the end of 1858, McQuilkin's weekly prayer meeting was becoming overcrowded. Multitudes wanted to join in the bold intercession. The fervent prayers focused on revival and the outpouring of the Holy Spirit. This wasn't the only gathering like this. Hundreds of others were being organized across Ulster.

Amid the profound intercession, the fire of revival would soon fall. The rising fervor was unprecedented in that generation. No one in Ulster had ever witnessed something so marvelous.

SUDDENLY THE FIRE FALLS!

On the evening of March 14, 1859, a crowd gathered at the largest church in Ahoghill for a prayer meeting. People crowded in, and so many were seated that officials feared the galleries would collapse. To accommodate the mass of people who were gathered they started moving some outside. People complied even though rain started to fall. They were so hungry for God that a storm couldn't turn them away. William Duewell, in his book *Revival Fire* tells us,

"They poured out into the street, and some three thousand people from all denominations—Presbyterians, Anglicans, Methodist, and Roman Catholic—were gripped by the Holy Spirit and stood as if paralyzed. A chilling rain fell on them, but the people knelt in the mud of the streets and prayed. A number of people were smitten down by the Holy Spirit that they lay prostrate in the mud."

William Gibson, fresh back from his trip to America, continues the story,

"Many convictions had taken place . . . Even strong men have staggered and fallen down under the wounds of their conscience, great bodily weakness ensues. The whole frame trembles . . . it is a heart-rending sight to witness... ringing of hands, streams of tears, and a look of unutterable anguish . . . they . . . appeal to the Lord for mercy with a cry of piercing earnestness . . . I have heard the cry as I have never heard it before."

In Ulster, heaven was touching earth. The revival spread like wild-fire across the region. All-night prayer meetings were held in virtually every town. Weeping, wailing, and singing could be heard on every street. Farmers abandoned their animals and crops. Clerks and businessmen put aside money-making and attended prayer meetings.

They held prayer gatherings in homes, barns, fields, schools, churches, businesses, and even along the city streets. Windows were cracked so those who could not enter could still hear the prayers and singing. Nothing could stop the Holy Spirit as the revival spread from town to town.

Ten thousand were saved when the revival hit Ballymena. Many of the families had not slept for days, afraid they would miss what God was doing. In other places, large open-air meetings of 25,000 people were held. One minister reported,

"The difficulty used to be to get the people into the church but the difficulty now is to get them out." Everything in the country was at a stand-still—with prayer on everyone's lips night and day.

Amazing things were transpiring as God moved. Numerous reports were circulated. James Bain, pastor of the Congregational Church at Staid, described what was happening around him,

> "Our Sabbath services are continuous, from nine in the morning until ten at night. We are engaged from nine to twelve in prayer meetings for the young, from twelve to two in public service, from two to four in prayer meetings, from five to eight in the evening service, and finally in our evening prayer meeting."

Christians felt a renewed hunger and earnestness in prayer. The breath of God was blowing across the country and the enemy bowed his knee. This stirring became known as the "1859 Ulster Revival," and in just one year produced 100,000 converts.

IRELAND AFLAME

The land of Ireland was now aflame, and extraordinary newspaper reports were coming from countryside. Daily reports were being made of the extraordinary move of God.

> LONDONDERRY—Several daily prayer meetings with 5000 or more attending.

> COLERAINE—united meetings with Presbyterians, Methodists, Independents, and Baptists. One minister was quoted as saying, "For the last three weeks it has been one continual Pentecost."

> BELFAST—every street blocked with prayer meetings. Crime is nonexistent; sinners, drunkards, and prostitutes all praying

together. Whole distilleries are closed. A "monster" open air prayer meeting held in Botanic Gardens.

CATHOLIC CHURCH—selling Holy water to protect their people from this "revival devil" . . . new work of the devil . . . an alarming contagious disease. Reliable experts testified that more Catholics converted in 1859 than in the previous fifty years.

DUNDROD—revival spreads "with the rapidity of a prairie fire." Groups praying around prostrate bodies of men and women... some are in trances, others crying for mercy... some sinking in a swoon... some staggering and dropping to their knees... others fleeing in terror from the scene.

DUNMILLS—six thousand prostrate before the Lord.

CLOUGHMILLS—one hundred prayer meetings in one town keeping revival fires burning.

BALLYCARRY—prayer meetings every night for 48 weeks continue until daybreak, with over one thousand attending.

CARRICKFERGUS—revival prayer meetings in salt mines hundreds of feet underground.

DERRY—intense sinners converted instantly pray prayers that are superior to those of ordained ministers. Children praying for unsaved adults.

BOROUGHSHANE—Holy Spirit falls over factory... all workers lying prostrate before the Lord. Factory closed for two days while people prayed.

THE IRISH YEAR OF GRACE

1859 was the "Irish Year of Grace." As a result, Northern Ireland became known, for a time, as the most peaceful province in the British Empire. "Revival Trains" loaded to capacity with travelers would sweep from city to city. Everyone on board would be praying and singing hymns. Entire schools were closed for days because of the reviving of the children for spiritual things.

The effects of the revival were astonishing. It would take several volumes to relate all the marvelous things God was doing in 1859. Historian Ian R. K. Paisley writes that in Ulster Revival,

> "Profanity, Sabbath profanation, and drunkenness are set aside. Many . . . [taverns] are closed, a cock-pit has become a preaching station and families, where nothing but vice in its worst forms could be seen, have been brought to love and adore the Lord."

REVIVAL IN THE BRITISH EMPIRE

As powerful as the Ulster Revival was, God was not finished. The heavenly fire continued to spread far and wide. The glory of God would soon cover the British Empire.

As the revival spread from Ireland to Wales, prayer meetings erupted. People awoke before the light of dawn and began lining the roads a half mile in every direction to intercede. In one Welsh city, over three thousand new converts joined the churches. Reflecting on what was transpiring in Wales, Thomas Phillips writes, "Every day is a Sabbath now. The people cannot think of anything but to feed their cattle and attend prayer meetings."

In 1860 the banner on a newspaper declared,

"REVIVAL OF THE SPIRIT OF PRAYER... CHRISTIAN
UNITY... MOST POWERFUL AWAKENING... HEAVENLY
FIRE... FINGER OF GOD."

In this part of the empire, God was transforming the hearts of
multitudes. By the end of the year, Wales saw one tenth of its
total population committed to Jesus. The Welsh Revival of 1859
was greater than what occurred in 1904-1905.

Neither Ireland nor Wales were alone in this ongoing
expansion of glory. The fervor spread to neighboring countries.
In glens of Scotland, the flames of the awakening were ignited. In
this time, over 300,000 souls were added to the Lamb's book of
life.

In England, the seat of government, this same revival brought
over 400,000 into the Kingdom. The impact was even felt in
Scotland and the outlying Hebrides Islands.

The fires of revival won't stay still. They keep moving and
burning every place where there is fuel. It wasn't long before
these flames were even carried to South Africa. A wonderful
outpouring of the Holy Spirit overwhelmed the Zulu and Bantu
tribes. Thousands of tribesmen and warriors traveled several
days to worship at mission churches. That which was called "The
Zulu Revival" launched hundreds of multi-day, continuous
prayer meetings. Tribes, two hundred miles away in Botswana,
were stricken by a move of the Spirit. Thousands were crying out
to have a relationship with the Lamb of God who took away their
sins.

THE GLORIOUS WORK IN 1859

In 1859, the hand of God was moving across the world. People
from many tribes and tongues were declaring that Jesus Christ
was Lord to the Glory of the Father. One minister said, "It was
worth living ten thousand ages in obscurity and reproach to be

permitted to engage in the glorious work of the last six months of 1859." Similarly, Thomas Phillips acknowledged, "It is questionable whether anything more powerful has been felt in America, Ireland, or Wales." An editor of Christian magazine affirmed:

> "I have never witnessed anything like what I now see daily. You hear of nothing but the revival. Ungodly people quake and tremble... some of the most ungodly men seemed to be entirely bewildered; they could hardly find their way home that night... Bless be God... many found their way to the blood of the cross."

The Third Great Awakening in the United States, the Ulster Revival, along with the other spiritual tributaries that spread around the world, were testimonies to one thing—prayer. As the people learned to fervently intercede, they encountered the glory of God in a way that they had never known. The Lord's goodness and power overwhelmed them.

Let us, in the modern church, re-embrace the power of prayer. Heartfelt intercession reconnects us to God and becomes a vehicle for releasing His wisdom and power. Of all the spiritual weapons given to us, prayer is the most powerful.

> "Ask of Me, and I will give You the nations for Your inheritance, and the ends of the earth for Your possession" (Psalm 2:8).

THE SHANTUNG REVIVAL

Marie Monsen, Norwegian Lutheran Mission

"God had only one Son, and He was a missionary."—David
Livingstone

"The Christian is not obedient unless he is doing all in his
power to send the gospel to the heathen world."—A. B. Simpson

"Untold millions are still untold."—John Wesley

"The history of missions is the history of answered prayer."—Samuel Zwener

"I cannot trust myself, for I am nothing. I cannot trust in what I have, for I have nothing; and I cannot trust in what I know, for I know nothing. It will not be hard for me to trust in Jesus."-Rodney "Gypsy" Smith

"The Holy Spirit poured over me just like water... wave after wave... this is my spiritual birthday! Although I already believed in Jesus since my childhood days, this new experience is a life-changing one for me."—John Sung

Genuine revival is a spontaneous movement of the Holy Spirit—not something orchestrated by flesh and blood. It is when God sovereignly breaks into history and entire nations are overwhelmed with His glory. The ancient prophet revealed the following: "But who can endure the day of His coming? And who can stand when He appears? For He is like a refiner's fire and like launderers soap" (Malachi 3:2).

In 1935, the Executive Secretary of the Baptist Foreign Mission Board, Charles E. Maddry, visited the North China Mission and reported the following back to the leadership in Richmond, Virginia:

"A glorious revival is sweeping Northern and Interior China, such as we have not seen in America in a hundred years. We have seen it and felt its power. It is a revival of fire and burning. Sin is being burned out of broken lives, and men and women are being absolutely made over. The power of Christ has come to grips with the power of satan and it is a fearful conflict. Satan has held sway and dominion over China for unnumbered and weary centuries. His kingdom is suddenly being challenged and broken by the power of a risen and enthroned Christ."

Maddry wasn't the only official observing this incredible stirring. A missionary arriving in China that same year was also shaken by what he witnessed,

"I have come into the midst of revival fires in China. Marvelous, wonderful, deep is the work of the Holy Spirit here. Oh, that the fire might fall amongst Southern Baptists of America. I came up to Hwanghsien from Tsining for a few days and I have never seen a place so transformed. The first delightful thing I noticed was the warmth and genuineness of the cordial welcome of the Chinese. They seem to have a baptism of love that flows out of their very countenances. The spirit of worship and praise and reverence in the church service Sunday surpassed anything I saw or felt in America."

The testimonies of this glorious move of God in China were striking because they came from Southern Baptist missionaries. Individuals from this tradition usually oppose the unusual manifestations of the Spirit. Those being affected in the revival experienced visions, trances, and dreams. As the repentant were responding to the Lord, they were trembling, speaking in tongues, and falling out under the weightiness of the Spirit. These were not the kinds of things you would typically see in a Baptist congregation.

In what many called "The Greatest Revival in Baptist History," conservative missionaries were advocating for "Pentecostal manifestations." They would not have used this terminology, but as the Lord moved, they had an openness to the "infilling of the Holy Spirit." The revival took many into places that they never expected.

What was transpiring in these missionary outreaches was contrary to the teachings of the Southern Baptist Convention. For years, this evangelical denomination closed ranks and stymied revivals, but this event was difficult to dismiss. The officials knew the missionaries were godly, Bible-believing Baptists. They were ordained and trained in their denominational seminaries. So when these men reported unusual phenomena, it was coming from insiders.

Unbelief turned to curiosity as reports arrived of the manifestations, power and unction taking place on the mission field. These men were shaken to the core like the Apostle Paul when he shouted,

> "Oh, the depth of the riches both of the wisdom and knowledge of God! How unsearchable are His judgments and His ways past finding out" (Romans 11:33)!

This revival was revolutionary. Not only was a pagan country being transformed in the magnificence of the Lord's presence, but this move of God also reawakened apathetic missionaries—reminding them of their divine calling. God brought in the lost and renewed His church. Everything became new in Christ.

Although the revival began small, in the Shantung providence, it spread throughout China and Manchuria. Some have suggested that it was the most important event in the history of world missions. It was an Asian awakening, but people still called it the "Shantung Revival."

AS MANY GODS AS TOWNS

In the early twentieth century, China was spiritually dead. The spirit of idolatry strangled the life out of many. The same critique that the Prophet Jeremiah had made applied to this nation: "You . . . have as many gods as you have towns" (Jeremiah 11:13). To the Chinese, the Christian God was merely another god in a pantheon of deities. They had little interest in adding anything else to their apathetic spirituality.

All of China was in turmoil—spiritually and politically. During the Nationalist Revolution, multitudes turned from God. They abandoned the Church because of severe persecution.

Many of the churches were sitting empty. The believers who remained were indifferent, with virtually no conception of morality.

Throughout the Chinese Church, there was no conviction of sin. Husbands who supposedly claimed the name of Christ often had sexual relations with concubines. It was not unusual for churchgoers to be high on opium or drunk. Many "Christian" families kept idols, representing ancestral gods, on the living room table, offering incense while intoxicated. There was little authentic Christian witness.

LETHARGIC MISSIONARIES

The reason things were so bad in China was because of the backslidden condition of the leaders. Missionaries rarely had any enthusiasm about their work. There was a focus on education, not evangelism. Also, mission agencies often sent humanists and theological liberals.

At this time, there weren't many indigenous churches. White missionaries started most congregations, and many of these men were racist and controlling. Most revealed their sense of superiority by their administration and condescending preaching. One seminary professor declared, "I have always felt a white face was superior to a yellow face."

The Chinese hated this attitude and developed their own negative opinions of the outsiders. Frustrated with the missionaries' heavy-handedness, they called them "foreign devils" and "the scum of the earth."

Spiritual conditions had gotten so bad that missionaries were leaving the field and giving up on their calling. Many abandoned their pursuit of God for lucrative business ventures and all that the world offered.

Mission boards recognized they were in trouble. The ministers were often in the same fallen condition as the ones they were ministering to. Their private lives and messages were mired in compromise. Those called to reflect Jesus had very little life or joy.

In one meeting, Southern Baptist officials gathered to discuss the discouraging condition in the churches. The leader stood up to resign, but before exiting, he said,

> "The sixty dead churches on the Ping-Too field have had their chance… after people… had given their lives in witnessing to the gospel all these years, the churches are still not able to stand and go forward on their own, perhaps they ought to be left alone, and the missionaries should go home or to some other field. I for one am so serious I'll be the first to go."

Many sensed that it was time for judgment to begin in the church (Peter 4:17). God's servants needed to repent and pray for His mercy to come upon them.

PRAYER MEETINGS

Some key leaders organized prayer meetings in Baptist mission stations, but they didn't know how to intercede. The men who gathered pleaded for revival and declared, "Lord, let it begin in me." There wasn't much fervor, but they didn't give up in their efforts.

The Lord increasingly moved upon prayers and there was a

renewed sense of unity. One of the Baptist missionaries in this group declared,

> "I know God has called me to China to preach… He has not withdrawn that call. It is true we need revival in the Chinese churches but somehow I feel that if we had the power as missionaries that He promised in Matthew 28:18 and then in Acts 1:8, the whole situation would be different. Giving up, going home or elsewhere is not the solution to our problem. Praying and holding meetings in the churches have not changed things much. I'm convinced what is needed, for our prayers to work, are missionaries to humble themselves, confess their sins, and let the Holy Spirit fill them. Revival ought to begin with us."

The prayer meetings began in 1921, but it would take another six years to see things shift. The missionaries knew they needed to be the first to come under the conviction of sin and make things right. Missionary, John Abernethy, wrote,

> "Before the evangelistic aspect of the revival came, the Church came under deep conviction of sin," and until the missionaries confessed their sins and restitution made, there would be no relief from the conviction power of the Holy Spirit."

Many of the missionaries cried out in agony about their sins in the middle of the prayer meetings. God was doing a tremendous work in the hearts of His servants. As long as they were "lost," they could not call the "lost." God was setting His Church right.

GOD'S SPARK

God was positioning China for revival and Marie Monsen, a veteran Lutheran missionary from Norway, would be one of the catalysts. One of her contemporaries said she was "one of the outstanding instruments God used for the reviving of the churches in Northern China... [Monsen] was in possession of a power from God that was well-nigh irresistible."

Monsen organized a series of meetings in Chefoo in 1927. This would be the spark that would turn Asia upside down and launch the "Great Pentecost."

Monsen's convicting sermons burned like a fire, and she surprised everyone when she directed her words toward fellow missionaries. She stood eye-to-eye with her colleagues and asked, "Are you born again?" Monsen wasn't afraid to bring a confrontation, asking them if they were filled with the Holy Spirit. She stood at the door at the back of the church after her messages and asked the leaders, on their way out, if sin was in their lives.

Her words cut deep, and the Holy Spirit used Marie to expose the fruitlessness and lethargy in the missionary work. Eyes were opened to the callousness and hard hearts. One said that her words "felt like the thrust of a sword," and another declared, "They were like lightening bolts." The spirit of repentance and travail gripped the foreign preachers and educators. A few were even saved for the first time. One leader wrote,

> "I knelt by the bed and prayed, 'Lord, I don't know whether I'm saved or not... I want to be right with you... please show me what is wrong.' My sins came before me like darkness and I cried... just then the burden rolled away and the Light of Salvation shone in my soul."

These men and women nailed unforgiveness, pride, compromise, and prejudice on the cross. Some were so impacted that they returned their Mission Diplomas because they had been a part of a cheating scandal. The missionaries were convinced that they needed the fullness of the Holy Spirit—a baptism of power. One wrote,

> "For several years there had been an increasing hunger in the hearts of most of us to see more of the power of the Holy Spirit in our work… We knew the doctrine of the Acts of the Apostles, but we were not experiencing it as we knew we should… so much of our work showed up as "hay and stubble" so that most of us were willing to 'Humble ourselves under the mighty hand of God that He might exalt us in due season.'"

Once the stains of sin were cleaned from their lives, prayers from the previous six years broke through. It was like they were experiencing an open heaven for the first time. Some of the affected men held a prayer meeting in Hwanghsein that continued, day and night, for four consecutive days. Everyone in that gathering came under the conviction of the Holy Spirit and started confessing their sins.

Marie preached to a group of Southern Baptist leaders in Chefoo, who had gathered for a time of spiritual renewal. They spent most of their time in prayer and Bible study. But as they interceded for a new awakening in China, an awareness of their own spiritual needs struck them and many broke out in tears.

Ola Culpepper, the wife of the Seminary president, suffered from a painful, degenerative eye disease. The doctors could do little to help except offer thick prescription glasses. Marie was persuaded to minister to Ola. Placing oil on her head and eyes, the Lutheran preacher interceded for healing. Ola immediately took off her glasses and her eyes never bothered her ever again.

Watching what God was doing, conviction fell in the room. Some began shouting, praying, and singing in loud voices. Joy beyond description filled the room and poured out into the community. China's spiritual awakening had begun.

The people's responses to the Baptist missionaries abruptly

changed. They once had stone-faced stares when they heard the preaching, but now hundreds were rushing the altars in repentance. The whole spiritual atmosphere had changed.

Monsen preached in the town of Dairen, and the desperate people cried out. Even this veteran Lutheran missionary had never witnessed so much hunger. Multitudes gave their lives to Jesus.

Earnest prayer was now a daily occurrence, and they held meetings two or three times a day. An unusual spiritual manifestation was transpiring among many of the Southern Baptist missionaries. They were being baptized in the Holy Spirit with the evidence of speaking in tongues. Although this was a spiritual gift that the denomination rejected as a viable modern experience, the revival participants gladly received it.

However, as the revival took on a Pentecostal nature, alarming reports were sent back to the Foreign Mission Board. The Southern Baptist Convention hierarchy was alarmed about what was occurring. Some missionaries hid the fact that they were speaking in tongues because they didn't want to be taken off the mission field.

The Chinese converts were also being touched mightily, with powerful manifestations in every gathering. Along with tongues-speaking, multitudes encountered holy laughter (Psalm 126:2). In the middle of sermons, some congregants groaned and fell to the ground. Some rolled up and down the aisles, and others jumped in exhortation. Spiritually dead churches were coming alive.

Signs and wonders became common. The sick were healed, demons cast out, and people had powerful visions. Opium addictions were broken. Ancestral idols were destroyed. Marginal Christians would be overcome in a trance and start boldly preaching and hundreds would repent.

John Sung, an evangelist used greatly in the revival, rejected the validity of speaking in tongues until he witnessed an inexplicable display of power. He heard a man speaking eloquently in unknown tongues who was being moved upon by the Lord.

John Abernathy, a Baptist missionary, began to speak in tongues and had the following to say:

> "Lord, I most have this power no matter what the cost. If You want me to speak in tongues, or if You want me to do anything else that I have despised in others, let me do it. I must have this power without which I cannot go on... This was a Baptist revival, or rather it was a New Testament revival... and the Pentecost's had nothing to do with it... these manifestations are not out of place... when the Holy Spirit is in it, one ceases to feel that it is out of place."

As the revival spread, other denominations became a part of it. Groups who criticized or refused to surrender to the work of the Spirit missed out on God's visitation. While the Southern Baptist missionaries celebrated the work, some other Evangelical groups criticized the "excesses," and had very little fruit in their missions.

BACK HOME

Back in the United States, multiple reports came into the SBC foreign mission board. Sadly, many of them were biased and wrong. Dr. Charles E. Maddry, the Executive Secretary, traveled to China to see what was happening with his own eyes. He visited several Baptist missionary stations and came across hundreds of people.

Wherever Maddry went, joy-filled new converts welcomed him. It really struck him when he heard the congregations singing, praying in concert, and speaking in tongues. He had witnessed nothing like this. It cut him to the heart as he encountered people being saved en mass, the sick being healed, and demons cast out in Jesus' name. Although unsettled by the weeping, trembling and falling out in the Spirit, Maddry discerned that these were works of God. He wrote back to the Mission Board,

> "I don't understand it. I would do it differently. But I am convinced it is real... In the great revival that has swept through North and Interior China... our missionaries have their feet on the solid rock of Christ Jesus and they are building gloriously on the foundation laid so deep and strong by those heroes and martyrs who preceded them."

Before traveling back to America, Dr. Maddry made a speech at the campus of Shanghi Baptist University. He highlighted the wonderment and joy of the Shantung Revival. In closing he said, "I came, I saw. I have been conquered!"

The Shantung revival continued for another ten years, touching thousands across the continent of Asia. God's power and mercy are transformative, turning the entire world upside down. Many changes were wrought in the overflow of this awakening. Prejudices faded and Chinese leaders took over as pastors in the mission churches. God brought new life in a dark place.

Years later, John Abernathy penned the following:

> "You've asked today what is the most important event in the history of world missions? The answer... would be the, Shantung Revival in North China... This spiritual awakening was not an evangelistic conference or crusade, but an awakening in which Christians, Chinese and missionaries alike were quickened by the Holy Spirit into new life, vision and activity. Sinners came under terrible conviction of sin. Proud Chinese, always afraid of losing face, were struck down with conviction...

Unconverted church members, yes, and preachers became new creatures in Christ. Christians were filled with the Holy Spirit and endued with power for living, and serving, yes, and dying... The revival broke down the wall of partition between the Chinese and missionaries. There was no more feeling of superiority on either side. The term 'foreign devil' was never heard again in places where revival has gone... many... ask us how the revival came. The revival came about as a result of earnest prayer by groups and individuals, faith in God, and repentance of sin... God poured out on the leaders and the churches the spirit of grace and supplication. There was a thirst after God such as we have never known before."

When men and women learn to pray, the light of God breaks into the darkest corners of the world. The Lord is ready to touch the nations with the goodness of the gospel.

"Call to Me, and I will answer you, and show you great and mighty things, which you do not know." (Jeremiah 33:3)

12

HEBRIDES REVIVAL

Duncan Campbell and the Intercessors

"Revival is a visitation of God's Spirit on His people, but an awakening is a time of such intense visitation that both Christian and non-Christian communities are affected. Revivals alter the lives of individuals. Awakenings alter the worldview of a whole people or whole culture."—Billye Brim

"Let us return to the basic things of the word of God and prayer and soul winning and revival. Let us pray, Oh God, send a revival. Let it begin in me."—Lee Roberson

"Prayer begets revival, which begets more prayer."—Jim Cymbala

"The coming revival must begin with a great revival of prayer. It is in the closet, with the door shut, that the sound of abundance of rain will first be heard."—Andrew Murray

"The average man is not going to be impressed by our publicity, our posters, or our programs, but let there be a demonstration of the supernatural in the realm of religion, and at once man is arrested."—Duncan Campbell

The Hebrides are a group of windswept islands forty miles off the coast of Scotland. As a buffer between the mainland and harsh Atlantic gales, the land is bleak and treeless. The inhabitants embrace isolation as a way of life, and make a living on weaving looms and peat bogs. Gaelic—not English—is the preferred tongue.

A magnificent revival erupted in the Hebrides in 1949 and God's glory overwhelmed the people. Reflecting on this powerful stirring, David Smithers writes,

"The price for heaven-sent revival has never changed. Before the floods of Holy Ghost conviction could sweep across the Isles of the Hebrides, strong men were broken before God, travailing in agony of prayer through the long hours of the night for months. To do this, in spite of the demands of home and work, these men had to make time for waiting before God! This is perhaps the greatest problem besetting us today. We have all the modern luxuries of life to make work easier and yet we cannot make time to pray! What a tragic paradox! Dr. Wilbur Smith very aptly stated the matter when he said: "I never get time to pray — I've always got to make it."

J. D. King, a pastor from Kansas City, journeyed to the Hebrides Islands over a decade ago to get a first-hand view of this wonderful outpouring. He gazed upon a house shaken off its foundations during an intense God-saturated prayer meeting. He was also privileged to sit with a few of the surviving participants. When asked about the possibility of another move of God in the Hebrides, one man answered, in a strong Scottish brogue, "I will know revival is coming when I hear the sound of broken prayer."

Broken prayer? Oh, that the modern Church would assault the heavens with this type of intercession. Broken prayer is desperate, aggressive, and agonizing. It is a sound that cuts to the heart and shakes things to their very foundation.

"O God, You are my God; earnestly will I seek You; my soul thirsts for You; my flesh longs for You in a dry and thirsty land where there is no water" (Psalm 63:1).

Travailing prayer stirs the heart of God. When the Lord hears cries like this, He will gladly "bow down His heavens . . . and come down" (Psalm 144:5).

The outcome of fervent prayer is revival God's way! Duncan Campbell, a key leader in the revival, reminded his listeners, in this atmosphere of intercession, "You met God on meadow and moorland. You met Him in the homes of the people. God seemed to be everywhere."

Intercession breaks open the door to magnificent things.

THE LAND OF REVIVALS

As isolated as these islands are, one would think that moves of God would be rare, but nothing could be further from the truth. God favored the Hebrides with several visitations:

- The Great Revival of 1820.
- The 1859 Revival.
- The Revival of 1900-01.
- The Revival of 1903-1913.
- The Revival of 1923.
- The Revival of 1939.

A hunger for revival gripped the hearts of many in the mid-twentieth century. In the 1939 stirring, there were no organizing figures. The fervent prayers of laymen carried it. Besides intercessory church gatherings, the spiritually hungry met in homes, town halls, even in stony, weather-beaten moors.

Although this revival waned with the onset of World War II, an intense hunger lingered. Many prayed that the Lord would fan the dying embers. They believed that the Hebrides Islands would, once again, burn with a blazing fire.

A SPIRIT OF PRAYER

After the war, many gathered three nights a week for cottage prayer meetings. For many, fervent prayer was a way of life. Moreover, as the spirit of God came upon the intercessors, many wanted to join their gatherings. One participant said, "We would listen for the buses crowded with people singing and climb aboard. We knew it was taking people to the prayer meetings."

Many of the intercessory gatherings outgrew the cottages and people were forced to pray outside. As the spirit of intercession gripped hearts, there was a confident expectation that what God had done before, He would do again.

Hunger was rising. God was doing something new, but to

many, the events of 1949 were merely a continuation of what occurred a decade before.

Donald John Smith, the teenage son of a blacksmith in Barvas, said, "There was a great spirit of prayer everywhere, and that was actually the beginning of the revival." Recounting experiences at this time, he went to work at the "smithy," and found his father already there. Every morning Smith saw his father, on his knees in prayer, at the anvil. A minister who visited wrote,

> "Wherever people worked, they prayed... out on the moor, caring for the cattle, they prayed. Prayer was not a burden to them, but a delight. They loved to pray; they were strained to pray."

This ongoing intercession was not new in '49. Prayer had consumed this Scottish island for decades. Sandy Mor, a participant in the revival, proclaimed,

> "There was a oneness of spirit as we engaged in prayer and an increased burden as we interceded for an outpouring of the Spirit in the community . . . there seemed to be a compulsion to pray, and we all felt it."

INTERCESSORS PEGGY AND CHRISTINE SMITH

Although many of the seasoned saints were crying out to the Lord, the young people turned away from the church. They were entangled in drinking, dancing, and fleshly enticements. A holy fire needed to be kindled because so many still lived in the dark.

Peggy and Christine Smith, elderly intercessors from Barvas, were burdened about the spiritual lethargy. Although one was blind and the other constrained with arthritis, both cried to God about the appalling state of religion in their parish.

Consumed with a passion for intercession, they held God to His word. The Lord said, "I will pour water on him who is thirsty and floods upon the dry ground" (Isaiah 44:3), and they believed it. Peggy proclaimed, "This is His promise. We believe that God is a covenant-keeping God who must be true to His covenant engagements. He has made a promise and he must fulfill the promise." She continued, crying out, "I will not let You go until You bless Barvas."

The sisters were so burdened with the needs that they spent three nights a week in prayer. They knelt from 10:00 pm to 4:00 am—lost in intercession for their homeland. As they prayed, they received a vision of their church crowded with young people and a strange minister in the pulpit. Struck by what the Lord revealed, they called for James Murray MacKay, the parish minister. The sisters said,

> "You must do something about it . . . I would suggest that you call your office bearers together and that you spend with us at least two nights in prayer . . . Tuesday and Friday if you gather your elders together, you can meet in a barn, and as you pray there, we will pray here."

This God-fearing man, knowing how intimate these women were with God, obliged their request. He gathered seven of the men from the parish church to pray with him. After a month and a half of intense travail, the youngest of the deacons was overcome with the glory of God. Feeling the stirring of the Spirit, he stood up and read Psalm 24,

> "Who shall ascend into the hill of the Lord? Who may stand in His holy place? He who has clean hands and a holy heart, who has not lifted up his soul to an idol nor sworn deceitfully. He shall receive blessing from the Lord."

Then, with tears in his eyes, he said, "It seems to me to be so much humbug to be praying as we are praying, to be waiting as we are waiting, if we ourselves are not rightly related to God."

This deacon lifted his hands and shouted, "God, are my hands clean? Is my heart pure?" Then he fell to the floor and entered into a trance. The other men were shocked and fell to their knees as the power of God swept through the parish. An awesome awareness of God and His holiness blanketed that small community.

The next day eternal things gripped the townspeople, and many were so gripped by God, they would rather go to the church than work. What had once been a few flickering embers had turned into a mighty flame. God was at work in the Hebrides again.

STRANGE MAN IN THE PULPIT

Intercession continued and the Holy Spirit quickened Peggy Smith to contact Reverend MacKay once more and share the following with him:

> "I think you ought to invite someone to the parish. I cannot give a name, but God must have someone in mind because in our vision we saw a strange man in the pulpit, and that man must be somewhere."

MacKay had plans to attend the Strathpeffer Convention, a leadership gathering on the mainland of Scotland. At this meeting, he reached out to Tom Fitch, a God-fearing evangelist, inviting him to minister on the island. MacKay said,

> "Won't you come for ten days; a ten day special effort. We've had so many of them over the past couple of years, but we feel

that something is happening in the parish and we would like you to attend."

Fitch said that he could not come, but he knew someone else that fit the bill. He said,

"I don't feel that I am the man, but quite recently there has been a remarkable move in Glasgow under the ministry of a man by the name of Campbell. I would suggest that you send for him."

Duncan Campbell, an evangelist tied to The Faith Mission, was renown for his bold revival preaching. In the late forties, he stepped away from the association to accept a position in three Presbyterian congregations.

This new arrangement didn't work out very well for Campbell. The pressures so discouraged him that he thought he might be out of the will of God. Sheena, Campbell's young daughter, asked, "Daddy, God used you in revival in the past; how is it that you are not seeing revival now?" This question devastated him. Campbell knew God was directing him back into an evangelistic work, so he resigned and returned to his former role at Faith Mission.

Campbell was a commanding preacher, and several congregations wanted him to minister. Pastors would contact the Faith Mission Headquarters to schedule him. So, Mackay reached out to the organization and invited Campbell to minister at the parish church in Barvas.

Percy Bristow, the Faith Mission General Secretary, told Campbell about the invitation, but since the calendar was already full, he recommended that the preacher decline the offer.

Campbell was uncertain. He sent a reply to Bristow in October 1949 with the following message:

"I have written to the Reverend James MacKay, Barvas, to say that I am not free to visit Lewis this winter, but hope to do so at a later date, if the door is still open. I take your decision as guidance in this matter, although I must say it goes against my own leading and judgment. I am however content to rest in your decision and leave the issues in higher hands."

When MacKay received the rejection letter from Campbell, he shared the disappointing news with Peggy and Christine. Undaunted, the sisters asked him to forward another message to the evangelist. MacKay agreed and sent off another heartfelt request.

Campbell answered the second letter, reiterating that it was impossible for him to come at this time. He was a featured speaker at a holiday convention and could not break free.

When Peggy received the news, she said, "That is what the man is saying, but God has said otherwise, and the man, whoever he is, is going to be here in ten days."

Peggy and Christine fell on their faces in intense intercessory prayer. They would not let up until the will of the Lord was firmly established. Duncan Campbell, at this moment, was seated on the platform in Northern Ireland, prepared to speak to the assembly. Suddenly, he felt an overwhelming impulse to leave at once and make his way to the Hebrides Islands.

Campbell stood up and left the platform, immediately, addressing no one in the room. He booked passage on a ship and made his way to Lewis, from the mainland of Scotland—a seven-hour trip on choppy, turbulent waters. Within ten days, just as Peggy prophesied, Duncan Campbell stood in Barvas.

Since he traveled to the Hebrides under the Holy Spirit's unction, Campbell hadn't had time to tell anyone that he was coming. When he stepped off the steamer, he didn't expect to find anyone waiting for him. Yet, on the pier, stood Reverend MacKay and two of his elders.

After a few pleasantries, one elder posed a question, "Mr. Campbell, I would like to ask you a question before you leave this pier: Are you walking with God?" He answered, "Well, I think I can say this: that I fear God." The elder put his hand on Campbell's shoulder and said, "That will do." Campbell realized that he was standing before men who had been touched by the hand of God.

A SOVEREIGN MOVE OF GOD

The Scottish preacher would be a pivotal part of guiding the revival in the months ahead, but it didn't ignite because of him. When Campbell arrived, the stirring was already underway. He observed, "God is already at work and the opportunity is great... it seems to me that we are on the verge of something grand and glorious here."

Campbell's powerful preaching would bring hundreds more into the work, but he was not the catalyst. Years later, he would write,

> "I would like to make it perfectly clear that I did not bring revival to the Hebrides. It has grieved me beyond words to hear people talk and write about the man who brought revival to the Hebrides... I didn't do that. Revival was there before I ever set foot on the island. It began in a gracious awareness of God sweeping through the parish of Barvas."

Genuine revival was and is a sovereign work of the Holy Spirit. No man will ever be able to bring it into existence through their fleshly exertions. In the Hebrides, like every other move of God, the Holy Spirit was the architect and sustainer of revival.

A STOP OFF BEFORE BED

When Campbell first made it to the Hebrides, he was exhausted from traveling on a train and ship all day. He hadn't had time to eat or prepare for the upcoming services.

When still at the shipyard, Reverend MacKay said,

> "I am sure that you are ready for your supper... and bed. But I wonder if you would be prepared to address a meeting in the parish church at 9 o'clock tonight... It will be a short meeting and then we will make for the manse and you will get your supper and your bed and rest until tomorrow evening."

Over three hundred people were waiting when McKay, Campbell, and the elders arrived at the church. The ensuing service lasted two hours—extremely short compared to the all-night prayer sessions over the previous month. In this meeting, people felt a gentle moving of the Holy Spirit, but it wasn't the explosion they were expecting.

Campbell gave the benediction at around 11 o'clock and was walking down the aisle to leave when one intercessor shouted, "God, You can't fail us! You can't fail us!" The young man fell to his knees and laid prostrate on the floor in a trance. Campbell proclaimed, "Here is a young man who knows God in a way that perhaps I do not. He speaks to God; could I speak to Him in that way?" Stunned by the intensity of this intercession, conviction shook Campbell.

SOMETHING WONDERFUL HAS HAPPENED

Before Campbell could leave the Barvas church, they could hear footsteps from outside and the door of the church swung open. A blacksmith ran in, shouting,

"Mr. Campbell, something wonderful has happened. Oh, we were praying that God would pour water on the thirsty and floods upon the dry ground and listen, He has done it! He has done it!"

Looking out the door, Campbell was astonished to see over six hundred people from across the parish coming from every direction—hills, roads, and old pathways. They were all making their way to the church. The preacher noticed all the car headlights, lanterns, and torches. People covered the whole terrain, coming as far as the eye could see. God had answered the prayers of His saints. As it was in the days of Isaiah, the Hebrides Islands were being awakened.

"It shall come to pass that before they call, I will answer; and while they are still speaking, I will hear." (Isaiah 65:24)

People already in bed for the night arose and dressed. Scores of men in taverns put down their drinks and left. The bar tenders and the owners of the saloons soon followed them.

People from all walks of life, some even from miles away, were quickened in their spirits. An unknown force compelled them to make their way to the church and make things right with God. But only one congregation had its lights on—the Barvas Church. So people were making their way there.

AS FLEEING FROM A PLAGUE

Even the youth were touched as the Spirit of God moved across the island. Over a hundred young people were attending a dance and their minds were far from the Lord. But God's power fell upon the revelers. All at once, one musician stopped playing and put down his instrument. He walked out, saying, "I am sorry, but I've got to get right with God!"

The music trailed off as other band members felt the conviction of the Lord. As they walked out, the emcee did as well. All that was left in the silence were the dancers, but the Spirit got a hold of them as well. Within minutes, the dance hall was empty.

One observer reported that, "everyone fled from the hall as fleeing from a plague." The convicted party-goers saw the lights in the Barvas church and made their way there. A hunger and a thirst gripped the masses. Now, over seven hundred people were surrounding the church.

When the doors of the church were opened, the crowd rushed in. Campbell had to elbow his way to the front. Lying prostrate, near the pulpit, was a young woman from the dance crying out, "Oh, God, is there mercy for me? Oh, God, is there mercy for me?"

This was the beginning of an ingathering of young adults. Many had turned from the faith of their fathers, but the revival quickened their hearts, bringing them back to the church.

AWE AT THE POLICE STATION

The revival gathering continued until four in the morning. Although they were dismissing people, many were still singing Psalms and interceding. Exhausted, Campbell wanted to find his lodging and get a little rest.

Yet as the preacher was leaving, a young man entered the sanctuary and said they needed him at the police station. When asked why, the young boy said, "Oh, there is nothing wrong, but there must be at least four hundred people gathered around the police station just now. All of them are on their faces seeking more of God."

Because no other church was open, the crowd went there— knowing the chief was a God-fearing man.

Donald John Smith, a fifteen-year-old touched by God weeks

before, stood before the people to pray. He clasped his hands together and uttered one word—"Father." Immediately, everyone was melted in tears as the Presence of God permeated the scene.

As Campbell and others walked toward the station, they passed young and old from every walk of life. Widows, shepherds, magistrates, and whole families were standing along the roadside praying, singing, wailing, and crying. The marvelous work of God taking place in Lewis was unmistakable.

Those encountering the Holy Spirit were immersing themselves in the study of scriptures like never before and entering into deeper realms of prayer. Campbell could sense the changes as he interacted with the Hebridean families.

The next day, he came to visit Donald, the teenager who prayed at the police station. He found him on his knees in a barn. In front of him was an open Bible. When Campbell entered, the boy said, "Excuse me a little, Mr. Campbell, I am having an audience with the King."

A COMMUNITY SATURATED WITH GOD

Within a short time, the presence of God also fell on neighboring communities and the churches became crowded morning and evening.

At one point, a sanctuary that seated a thousand people was standing-room-only at three in the morning. Hundreds stood outside—praying and listening—because there was no room inside. Inside resembled a battlefield with hundreds prostrate on the floor and many slumped over the pews weeping.

The church services began to change in the wake of the revival. Prepared sermons were discarded and preachers spoke extemporaneously. Psalm singing took on an even greater fervor.

When the services ended, crowds did not want to leave. Individuals lingered at the church or traveled to nearby homes to continue fellowshiping. Many sang and prayed long into the early morning hours. Work seemingly stopped for a while. From sun rise to sun rise, eternal things were all that the people focused on.

There was no stopping this expanding move of God. It spread across the Hebrides like an out of control wide-fire. Thousands of lives were changed as the people from various parishes came together to pray.

In this astounding revival, worldly pursuits fell by the wayside. Taverns were closed and they found former drunkards praying for the continuance of the revival several times a week. God was doing astounding things. Colin and Mary Peckham wrote,

> "No church building was big enough, so overflow meetings had to be arranged . . . Buses, vans and cars brought the people, and crowds gathered around unable to get in. Word had to be sent to one district to stop the buses, but even then the people gathered and stood outside for three hours . . . in the midst of a snowstorm. There was a mighty manifestation of the power of God in the meetings . . . Wave after wave of the Holy Ghost's power swept over the meetings and strong men were broken down and crying for mercy . . . several have come to know the Lord who were miles away and not in contact with any of our meetings. The entire district is in the grip of revival!"

The magnificence and wonder of what God was doing in these islands cannot be overlooked. The Spiritually dead were being reawakened and the heart of intercession was reinvigorating the church. Nancy Leigh DeMoss, a revival historian, observed,

> "People could not sleep and houses were lit all night. People walked the streets in great conviction; others knelt by their bedsides begging for pardon . . . so great was the supernatural moving of God that most of the homes did not escape the

unction of the Spirit, and the routine of business stopped, that the islanders might seek the presence of God... the town was changed, lives and homes transformed and the fishing fleet, as it sailed out into the bay took with it a Precentor (musical director) to lead them in prayer and worship singing."

GOD'S SECRETS

Although the revival spread through several villages on the Isle of Lewis, it bypassed Stornoway—the governmental seat. Several ministers in this entry port city opposed the revival. Donald John Smith acknowledged, "The break between the churches was very sad, and damaged the spirit of the revival."

Around this time, Peggy, the blind intercessor, received a vision from God of seven unrepentant men from an isolated village. She saw them being gloriously saved and becoming pillars in the church of her fathers.

She sent for Campbell, recounting the vision and asking him to hold a meeting in that village. However, the people of that hamlet spoke against the revival. Campbell was reluctant, explaining to Peggy he had no leading to go there. There was no church, and the superintendent wouldn't allow the school to be used for a revival service. He told Peggy she was wasting her time and that he "doubted her wisdom in this thing."

Peggy turned toward Campbell—her sightless eyes piercing his soul—saying, "Sir, if you were living as near to God as you ought to be, He would reveal His secrets to you also."

Campbell received her terse rebuke and acknowledged the matter should be taken up in prayer. He said, "Peggy, would you mind if I call Reverend MacKay? And together we will spend the morning with you in prayer." Peggy nodded with her approval and together they knelt to pray—two ministry stalwarts and an 84-year-old blind intercessor.

After the men interceded, Peggy lifted her eyes toward the heavenly throne and declared,

> "Lord, you remember what you told me this morning, that in this village you are going to save many souls, but especially seven men who will be pillars in the church of my fathers. I am just after telling your servant, Mr. Campbell, but he is not prepared to accept it. Oh, Lord, give him wisdom because the man badly needs it!"

After hearing these words, Campbell was reminded that Peggy truly knew God and he should listen to her. So the preacher asked what time he should go to the village. She said, "Tomorrow at seven o'clock and God will already have the people gathered."

The next day, Campbell took five men to this hamlet and discovered that some men had gathered in a bungalow. The little home was so overcrowded that the Scottish preacher and his team could not enter. So Campbell went over to a small hill nearby and preached from Acts 17:30, "Truly, these times of ignorance God overlooked, but now commands all men everywhere to repent."

After preaching for a few minutes, Campbell was interrupted and told that he needed to return to the bungalow. Men were there who "are afraid they will go mental. They are in such a state! They are mighty sinners and they know it."

Coming through the front door, Campbell observed seven men prostrate and wailing on the floor—exactly as Peggy saw them. He spoke to the men and helped them repent before God. These new believers went on, as the old intercessor revealed, to be pillars in the Scottish church.

THE HOUSE THAT SHOOK

Campbell and his team were later invited to Arnol, a small community just outside of Barvas. This hamlet was also opposed to the revival. Despite the opposition, a prayer meeting was called and about seventy gathered to intercede for revival.

As they prayed, the spiritual atmosphere felt dry and hard. The revivalists wanted to experience a breakthrough, but the meeting went absolutely nowhere. Their earnest prayers seemed to fall to the ground. But Campbell and his crew refused to give up.

Around one o'clock in the morning, Campbell turned to Donald John Smith, the devout blacksmith, and asked him to close out the meeting with a prayer of acclamation. Smith was quiet the whole night, merely weeping and travailing before the Lord. After the preacher invited him to pray, he stood up, looked to heaven, and proclaimed:

> "God, do You not know that Your honor is at stake? Your honor is at stake! You promised to pour water upon him who is thirsty and send floods upon a dry ground and God, You are not doing it. It is not happening. There are five ministers in this meeting and I don't know where a one of them stands in your presence, not even Mr. Campbell, but I know my heart and I am desperately thirsty. You promised to pour on him who is thirsty. If you don't do it, how can I ever believe You again? You are a covenant keeping God. I challenge You, in all Your glory, to fulfill your covenant engagement."

After Smith uttered these words, the house shook violently. From the other end of the house, plates and cups shattered into fragments as they fell to the floor. A jug from the cupboard was also smashed in the shake up. All the walls shook and pieces of plaster fell to the floor.

Unbelievers, Christina Campbell and Donald Macleod, had fallen asleep during the lengthy prayer meeting but were jolted awake with the shaking. Because of what they encountered, they began weeping and wailing—pleading with the Lord for their salvation.

Reverend Murdo Maclennan, who was praying alongside the group, shouted, "Mr. Campbell, it is an earthquake!" But outside, everything was quiet. Only the granite house in Arnol was being affected. But the tremblings were so violent that it knocked the edifice off its foundation and remains so to this day; a monument to powerful "revival praying."

After this shaking, it was 2:20 in the morning and a shout went up, "look outside." The whole village was stirred! The roads and bogs were crowded with people carrying chairs asking, "Is there room for us in the churches?" Revival swept through Arnol as masses flocked to meetings night after night.

God was doing an amazing work in the Hebrides Islands. Soon Duncan Campbell traveled from parish to parish, stoking the revival fires in Ness, Carloway, Lochs, and Point. Wherever he went, people were converted. Describing what was happening, the Scottish preacher said that they were,

> "A community saturated with God . . . The presence of God was a universal, inescapable fact: at home . . . at the church and by the roadside . . . many who visited Lewis . . . became vividly conscious of the spiritual atmosphere before they reached the island."

CONTINUING INFLUENCE

The impact of the Hebrides Revival of 1949-1953 continued long after the fervor waned. The compelling story of this move of God impacted people around the world and stirred fresh longings for revival. Many prayed, "Let us be like the Hebrides."

Aspects of the revival were carried forward in other ways. Mary Anne Smith MacLeod, niece of Peggy and Christine Smith and cousin of Donald John Smith, moved away from the Hebrides Islands in the 1930s. She immigrated to America and fell in love with a gentleman named Frederick Trump. The two married in 1936.

Peggy and Christine Smith mailed a Bible to Mary Anne that was carried during the revival. Years later she gave that beloved Bible to one of her sons—Donald John Trump. He went on to become the 45th President of the United States. Providentially, the Bible from that mighty revival was utilized in his swearing in ceremony in 2017.

Did a tiny spark from this glorious Scottish awakening influence American history? There are many fascinating intersections that deserve further exploration.

THE SOUNDS OF BROKEN PRAYER

Peering back into the annals of the mid-twentieth century, what occurred in the Scottish Hebrides was astounding. The Lord reignited the hearts of the intercessors and set the whole island on fire. It awakened many to the reality of heavenly glory. Duncan Campbell later wrote,

> "At Pentecost God set the Church at Jerusalem on fire, and the whole city came to see it burn. I tell you that if that happened in any church today, within three hours the whole town would be out to see the burning, and they would be caught in the flames. It is fire we want. Yes, the best advertising campaign any church or any mission can put up is fire in the pulpit and flames in the pews."

What God did off the coast of Scotland inspires many to cry out for revival. As Donald John Smith suggested in 2010, when

God hears broken prayers, He will not withhold His glory. May we become like those who prayed for a fresh outpouring in 1949 and received it.

> "Oh, that You would rend the heavens! That You would come down! That the mountains might shake at Your presence."
> (Isaiah 64:1)

13

BROWNSVILLE REVIVAL (PART ONE)

Evangelist Steve Hill

"Giftedness and empowerment are not necessarily an endorsement of one's theology or character. God often moves in spite of us."—J. D. King

"Such hunger to have more of God was in my heart that I prayed for five hours a day for two-and-a-half years... the Spirit said to pray more . . . I increased my hours of prayer to seven and prayed on."—William Seymour

"We are too busy to pray, and so we are too busy to have power. We have a great deal of activity but we accomplish little; many services but few conversions; much machinery but few results."
—R. A. Torrey

"Reformation is the return to the sound doctrine of the Bible. Revival is the practice of that sound doctrine under the power of the Holy Spirit."—Francis Schaeffer

"Something deep inside of me was calling out to the deep of God and I said Lord there's got to be more."—John Kilpatrick

Both revivals and falling away occurred throughout the early Twentieth Century. The Pentecostal Outpouring and many other stirrings awakened countless souls.

But near mid-century, much of the church fell away again. People were backslidden and lethargic. But just as in days of old, the Holy Spirit once again purged and renewed the people. Visitations of the Lord were widely reported throughout the world.

In 1949-1953, God poured His glory over the Hebrides Isles off the coast of Scotland. The land was so saturated with the Lord's glory that people could feel the living, breathing presence of God in every glen. One unbeliever reported, "I haven't been to a church, but this revival is in the air everywhere. I can't get away from the Spirit."

The work of the Lord wasn't just transpiring in Europe. In the

United States, thousands were saved and healed. The lame, deaf, and blind were restored in the Salvation-Healing Revival (1946-1955). William Branham, Jack Coe, A. A. Allen, Oral Roberts, and T. L. Osborn—anointed evangelists—traveled the country hosting massive healing meetings. Tens of thousands reported marvelous breakthroughs.

In the late 1960s and 70s, the Woodstock generation was entangled in immorality and drugs. But the hippies and societal dropouts were awakened in a revival called "The Jesus Movement." Ten of thousands walked away from the darkness and gave their lives to Jesus. The newly revived broadcasted the good news across alleys and back roads of North America.

Around the same time, a fresh stirring emerged in the Mainline and liturgical churches. Roman Catholics, Episcopalians, Lutherans, and many from the older denominations were swept into a new move of the Spirit known as the Charismatic Renewal.

Each of these revivals were God-birthed visitations. The intense worship, radical manifestations, and message of freedom swept millions into the Kingdom of God. Jesus, as always, was preparing the remnant for something greater.

Revivals often have a rise and a fall. In the late 1970s and early 80s, some felt that the Jesus Movement and the Charismatic Renewal were waning. The Church was beginning to be distracted by technology and the pursuit of wealth. Many "revivalistic" churches had grown exponentially, but forgot what had been the basis for their successes. As always, God had a plan to turn everything around.

MOTHER'S DAY REVIVAL

In the late 1970s, John Wimber, a former rock-n-roll music producer, got saved and started working with the Calvary Chapel in Southern California. This fellowship was the hub of the Jesus

Movement. Wimber led hundreds of hippies and flower children into the Kingdom of God.

Later, Wimber became more closely associated with the Association of Vineyard churches, an emerging fellowship. This group was more open to gifts of the Spirit than the Calvary Chapel. Many could sense that there was something more on the horizon.

Lonnie Frisbee, one of the key leaders in the Jesus Movement, was invited to be a guest speaker at Wimber's church on Mother's Day 1980. He shared his testimony and invited the Holy Spirit to overwhelm all who gathered. Frisbee said, "The Church has, for years, grieved the Holy Spirit, but He's getting over it! Come, Holy Spirit!" After he finished, hundreds rushed to the altar and were overcome by the weightiness of His glory. Shawn Bolz, who was in this service, proclaimed:

> "I looked at my family as the first wave of the Holy Spirit was resting on many people. My mom and dad were terrified-like probably half of the congregation! They had never seen power like this. Then some of the high school kids got hit by this wave of the presence of God. My parents weren't sure, like many other leaders that night. At this point people all around the room were amazed-knowing it wasn't fake."

Thereafter, a move of the Holy Spirit broke out among the Vineyard Churches—affecting thousands across Southern California and other parts of the United States. Wimber and his colleagues were adept at ministering to conservative Evangelicals. Many who had been opposed to Pentecostals and Charismatics became open to the deeper work of the Holy Spirit.

Wimber instituted a controversial "Signs and Wonders" course at Fuller Theological Seminary, published Power Evangelism and hosted ministry conferences that drew in

Presbyterians, Baptists, and Methodists. This new move of God swept in thousands of "Empowered Evangelicals."

The full ramifications of what God was doing through this movement has yet to be explored.

THE ARGENTINE REVIVAL

While fires were sparking in the United States, God was also igniting a mighty work in Latin America. God often lights fires in unexpected places. No one imagined that Argentina, a land steeped in voodoo, witchcraft, and spiritualism, would be on the front lines of the next move of God.

American Evangelist Tommy Hicks, a leader in the Salvation Healing Revival along with other Charismatic leaders, made inroads in Argentina in the second half of the Twentieth Century. God also used deliverance-minded evangelists like Omar Cabrera. Things were changing in Argentina, but there was a need for a greater stirring.

In the 1980s, God used Carlos Annacondia, a business man tuned evangelist. He barely knew what he was doing, but he was faithful to the call. Whatever embers remained from the earlier decades were fanned into a raging fire. People called this marvelous awakening "The Argentine Revival."

Mass conversions were the norm wherever Annacondia preached. In the city of Mar del Plata, over eighty-thousand professed faith in Christ and thousands were delivered from demonic oppression. This bold Argentine evangelist would raise his hand and say, "Listen to me, Satan! In the name of Jesus of Nazareth, I command you to loose the captives, now!" Immediately, a wave of the Spirit would move over the crowd, exposing evil spirits. As they manifested, Annacondia and his anointed team would drive out every one in the name of Jesus.

The Argentine revival became a global phenomenon, attracting not only the spiritually hungry but also desperate ministers. Three men who visited this revival in the years to come were Randy Clark, John Arnott, and Steve Hill. These mighty men would set North America on fire.

RODNEY HOWARD-BROWNE

Leaders were being raised up in other parts of the world as well. In the 1980s, God quickened the heart of a young South African evangelist. Although emerging from a Word of Faith background, he pioneered some new ministry expressions. Howard-Browne ministered in what he liked to call "supernatural joy." Multitudes were overcome with laughter in his meetings. The Lord brought the recipients into a place of deeper commitment and love.

At this time, the church was regimented and precept-oriented. The teaching movement of the 1970s and 80s turned audiences into students and knowledge seekers. Many listeners were more caught up in doctrinal assertions than having ongoing Holy Spirit experiences. Dead religious forms had become too prominent in Charismatic circles. Howard-Browne's anointed messages on joy and freedom set thousands free.

As this South African evangelist burst on the scene, many did not know what to do with him. The overwhelming laughter that his audience encountered seemed out of place to older leaders. They thought the church should cry instead of seeking joy.

Howard-Browne had some breakthrough meetings in Lakeland, Florida, at Carpenter's Home Church. Thousands attended these services and experienced renewal. One participant said, "When I went to Howard-Browne's meetings, I wasn't sure if it was truly revival, but I could sense that God was up to something new."

RANDY CLARK

In the late 1980s, a Midwestern Baptist pastor came into contact with John Wimber at a James Robinson conference. He didn't know what to do with the teaching, but it captivated him. He asked for a Vineyard team to minister at his church and a revival erupted. This pastor's name was Randy Clark.

Clark's Baptist Association did not like what was transpiring, so he aligned with the Vineyard. As he met with Wimber and the national leaders, God disclosed He was going to accomplish a powerful work through him. But a decade passed and this promise never seemed to come to pass.

In 1993, Clark was desperate. He had launched a new Vineyard congregation in St. Louis, Missouri that hadn't grown as fast as he hoped and he felt dry. Clark had heard that Rodney Howard-Browne was ministering at Rhema Bible Church in Tulsa, Oklahoma. He wanted a fresh touch but didn't want to receive it from a Word of Faith church.

In many ways, the Vineyard was the antithesis of the Word of Faith Movement. Following the style of John Wimber, most of California-based ministers were low key. They de-emphasized striving in prayer. Clark felt that the Tulsa-rooted ministry was too heavy-handed. He didn't want to go to Rhema, but he was so hungry, he would go anywhere. Sometimes God uses the things that offend to reveal the condition of our hearts.

Clark traveled to Tulsa and sat through the Howard-Browne meetings. During the gatherings, God revealed to Clark that he had a distorted view of Word of Faith ministers. the Lord confronted him about his ungracious spirit. Clark knew he had to get into the prayer line and receive from those he once questioned.

As soon as Howard-Browne laid hands on Clark, he felt power race through him. He felt freedom and a fresh infusion of power. Clark said, "I could feel the power in my hands . . . I never had that before." With this spiritual impartation, Clark's destiny was about to be unlocked.

JOHN ARNOTT AND THE TORONTO BLESSING

John Arnott aligned with the Vineyard Movement several years after a fresh touch from God in the Charismatic Renewal. He attended Kathryn Kuhlman meetings and witnessed wonderful stirrings of the Spirit. He carried the fervor of that era into his later ministry endeavors. Arnott and his wife, Carol, were expecting an explosive revival to take root in North America.

Arnott labored to build a vibrant ministry in Ontario, Canada, but had seen little fruit. Like Randy Clark, he was tired and dry. In the early 1990s, he traveled to Argentina to receive a fresh impartation from the revival that was stirring there. Arnott felt like everyone was being touched in the stadium but him. He wondered, "What's wrong with me?"

In the fall of 1993, Arnott heard from Happy Lehman, a Vineyard regional leader, that Randy Clark had received a fresh touch from the Lord. He explained that many were being overwhelmed by the power of God and laughing as he ministered. Lehman's remarks intrigued Arnott, so he reached out to Clark and invited him to travel to Canada.

Clark got off the plane to minister at the Toronto Airport Christian Fellowship on January 20, 1994. That evening, the entire congregation was unshackled as the Spirit of God danced through the room. As hundreds of bitter people were overcome by joy, the "Toronto Blessing" was birthed.

As the services erupted, people continued to gather night after night. People weren't just laughing and being overwhelmed, they were also being healed and delivered. The manifestations were intense—shaking, trembling, and intense laughter. The phenomena in the meetings were controversial to outsiders. It would be hard to explain it all, but thousands claimed to be getting free and becoming more committed to Jesus than ever before.

Word spread and hundreds of thousands of people attended the Toronto meetings from around the globe. Myriads were discovering the joy of the Lord and learning about the love of the Father.

What began in Toronto spread to other places around the globe. This powerful, Spirit-led renewal was bringing many into the Kingdom and reigniting many burnt out ministries.

HOLY TRINITY BROMPTON ANGLICAN CHURCH

In the late 1980s and early 90s, the Vineyard Movement had already been making an impact in the Anglican Church. Dozens of congregations tied to the Church of England were praying for the sick and inviting the deeper work of the Holy Spirit. John Wimber's many trips to Europe had made an enormous impact.

Several churches in the United Kingdom were intrigued by what was transpiring at the Toronto Airport Vineyard Fellowship. Various leaders began to make the trans-Atlantic flights to see for themselves what was occurring. Most of them would be radically shaken and set on fire.

One of the English leaders touched in Toronto was Eleanor Mumford. At the time, she helped lead the South West London Vineyard Church. She carried this newly lit flame back to England. After returning, Mumford was invited to speak at Holy Trinity Church, an Anglican congregation in Brompton, England. At the end of her heartfelt message, the congregation was swept to the floor as if overcome by a hurricane gale. The same fire that had been lit in Toronto was now smoldering in England.

In the months that followed, the British began experiencing the freedom and joy of the Lord. Broken marriages were restored and people with emotional and psychological traumas were healed. Many were being awakened to the grace and mercy of

Jesus. The overwhelming love of the Father was transforming countless individuals.

EVANGELIST STEVE HILL

Soon, others were swept up into this burgeoning move of God. One of these firebrands was missionary-evangelist Steve Hill. After a troubled life of drugs and incarceration, he fell in love with Jesus and turned his life around.

After going through the Assemblies of God's Teen Challenge Program, he gained his footing. Hill ended up in Lindale, Texas, where several revival-minded Christians had gathered from around the United States—Leonard Ravenhill, David Wilkerson, Keith Green, Michael Brown, and others. These men gathered to pray and seek the Lord. The seeds of their prayers would bloom in the decades to come.

Later Hill and his wife moved to Argentina. He could learn from the mass evangelism practices taking place in that revival. He took part in many stadium events, learning the tone and techniques of the Latin American crusades. The robust spirituality of Annacondia, Cabrera, and others also affected him. This impassioned preacher was destined to be a revivalist.

Hill and his wife Jeri made their way back to the United States and began to itinerate. News about Rodney Howard-Browne's controversial meetings and the joy at the "Toronto Blessing" was spreading through the ministry circles. Some thought it was wonderful, but others questioned its legitimacy. Hill was just hungry for more.

With the interest in what was happening in Toronto, ministers were also discussing the overflow of that revival.

What was occurring in Toronto spread to other ministries and they began to have similar breakouts. One of the fresh sparks of this revival was lit in the United Kingdom. Many had carried the overflow across the Atlantic. Reading about this, Hill was drawn in like never before.

Since Hill would soon travel through London on a missions trip, he planned to stop off at *Holy Trinity Brompton* and witness the move of God firsthand. Vicar Sandy Millar was a friend. So the American evangelist arranged for a personal meeting. Hill wanted Millar to answer some questions and help him understand the emerging revival.

When Hill landed at Heathrow Airport in London, Holy Trinity Brompton had already been immersed in the revival for a year. People were laughing and trembling under the glory. Many would have overwhelming encounters as they fell in love with Jesus.

As Hill walked through the door of Holy Trinity Brompton, he witnessed scenes he didn't expect to see in an Anglican church. Among other things, he saw five hundred people laid out on the floor in spiritual distress. The tangible presence of God gripped the entire room.

Hill stood there in shock. This was more intense than anything he witnessed in Argentina. As Millar approached, the evangelist said, "Forget the meeting, just lay hands on me." The Vicar did, and Hill collapsed to the floor under the intensity of the Spirit's power. The evangelist laid motionless for forty-five minutes as stream after stream of the river of God flowed through him. Hill was never the same after what he encountered in England. Revival was burning in his soul.

PASTOR JOHN KILPATRICK

In the early to mid-1990s, there was talk of a spiritual awakening in the United States, but not much of it was coming from the Pentecostal sectors. Those who had been carriers of revival for decades had grown weary. Erecting sanctuaries, expanding bus ministries and Sunday school programs, had drawn many congregations away from the fires of revival. Something had to be done.

John Kilpatrick, the pastor of the twelve-hundred member Brownsville Assembly of God in Pensacola, Florida, enjoyed marvelous experiences with God when he was younger. Although growing up in poverty, God met with him on numerous occasions.

As a young man, Kilpatrick attended a prayer meeting with seventeen mature believers. In one meeting, an angelic visitation shook them. The glory and power of the Lord filled the room as the heavenly messengers surrounded them.

This awe-inspiring encounter lit a fire in Kilpatrick to seek God with all his heart and never give up until he received a blessing. As he matured and entered the full-time ministry, he was committed to taking people to a deeper place with God.

Kilpatrick was never satisfied with church as usual. He hated dead religion. He prayed for a sovereign move of God for years and never stopped contending for something more substantial to take place at his church. One time Kilpatrick said,

> "If people are to be saved, let's see them saved. If people need to be healed then, bless God, let's see them healed. If demons needed to be cast out I want to see it."

Like thousands of other pastors in the early 1990s, Kilpatrick heard reports about various outbreaks of the Holy Spirit around the world. People were discussing the revivals sweeping Argentina, Lakeland, Toronto, and England. Lives were being touched, but many felt that these meetings were bizarre.

The unusual phenomena inflamed Kilpatrick's personal biases. By his own admission, he could be judgmental and controlling. Over the years, Kilpatrick had been critical of "emotionalism." So, the reports of the strange manifestations in the emerging revivals were unsettling to him. Kilpatrick didn't like the laughter or other displays.

The staff at Brownsville Assembly of God discussed what was transpiring in Toronto and other places. They asked, "Why not us?" "What do you think?" "Is it God?" "Could these things be really happening?" They wondered whether this was a genuine move of God or a display of religious fanaticism? Kilpatrick maintained some lingering doubts.

One morning, in prayer, Kilpatrick heard God say, "John, if you don't get rid of your critical spirit, I'm going to have to pass you by." These words shook him to the core. The next day, plans were made to go to Toronto and encounter what was happening there.

Kilpatrick and his wife, Brenda, along with other Brownsville leaders, only made it as far as Nashville. While in transit, the pastor experienced an episode with his heart. As the hospital team was examining him, he encouraged his wife and team to continue on to Canada. Kilpatrick returned home alone.

When Brenda and leadership team returned, they were beaming. They recounted all the marvelous things they witnessed. Everyone who went to Toronto was radically changed. One of them told Kilpatrick, "Pastor, we don't understand it? We don't know what it is? But we know it is of God."

A holy desperation—a righteous jealousy—gripped Kilpatrick. He spent the pre-dawn hours at church alone, calling out with a loud wail in the darkness. The pastor exclaimed,

> "Oh God! There's got to be more. Thank You for this church, thank You for the people, thank You for my family but there's got to be more! I need You Lord. I'm dying inside. We have got to have more of You. If You don't come, I can't continue. I need You or I will die. More Lord, more!"

PREPARATION AND CRISIS

Kilpatrick genuinely wanted to encounter a fresh move of God. So he taught on revival preparation, instructing people on what they needed to do to get ready for a move of God. Amid this training, one topic gripped the congregation—controlling their tongues. Kilpatrick emphasized that the congregation needed to speak blessings instead of curses. He also sensed that this message was important for him to apply in his life as well. The whole church needed to change the way they thought and spoke.

At this time, Kilpatrick set out to increase interest in intercession. Weekly prayer meetings were organized in homes and at church. The Sunday night service at Brownsville incorporated ten prayer banners that the members gathered around and used to focus their intercession. Each had a different topic, but Kilpatrick noticed that most of the wailing and travail took place around the revival banner. This was what the church needed to focus on. Some were uncomfortable with this emphasis, but a majority were happy to begin the pursuit of revival.

The spiritual atmosphere was increasing and fallow ground was being tilled, but revival had not yet arrived.

By the early summer months of 1995, an unexpected crisis was arising. Along with Kilpatrick's incessant pastoral duties, a personal health crisis, and fatigue, he faced unexpected opposition from a few families in the congregation. A handful of prominent people urged him to move away from his prayer focus. They didn't believe that the church should be continually in pursuit of revival. They made it clear if Kilpatrick didn't change things, they would leave.

To make matters worse, Kilpatrick's beloved mother—a gracious woman who raised him alone—died unexpectedly. Throughout his life, she had been her son's rock and his emotional support. But now she was gone, and Kilpatrick had a hard time reconciling himself to this reality.

Kilpatrick was physically, emotionally, and spiritually drained. He did not have the stamina to take on another attack from the enemy.

On Wednesday, June 14, 1995, four days before Father's day, Kilpatrick and his wife met with Elmer Melton, the lead elder. The pastor said that he had no fight left. So, for the sake of the church, he thought it would be best if he resigned. Melton listened to his weary pastor's pleas and then he prayed:

> "Lord, we are here in the office of pastor Kilpatrick and he is in an awful way. We need a touch from You, we need Your wisdom and spiritual understanding. He has been faithful to You in all things. Revive us with revival! Strengthen him in his time of need. We surrender ourselves to You."

Kilpatrick appreciated Melton's words and agreed to finish out the month. He wasn't sure how he would do this, but he knew the Lord was faithful.

THE INVITATION

Months earlier, Kilpatrick had invited his long-time friend, Steve Hill, to preach in the evening service on Father's Day.

When Hill arrived in town on Saturday, June 17, 1995, Kilpatrick and his wife met with him at a restaurant. Freshly touched at Holy Trinity Brompton, the evangelist was ablaze. Brenda, Kilpratrick's wife, shared how she was wonderfully affected in Toronto. The two beamed with the stories of God's power and love.

Kilpatrick listened to Hill and his wife their recount marvelous experiences. But he didn't want them to know he was frustrated about missing out on the glory—"jealous-hearted."

Kilpatrick couldn't believe that he was burnt out, while his wife and ministry colleague were ablaze with fire.

Emboldened, Kilpatrick did something uncharacteristic; he invited Hill to speak in the morning service at Brownsville Assembly of God. This was an unusual request. Kilpatrick rarely turned over his pulpit on Sunday mornings—particularly Father's Day.

When Hill heard this offer, he was stunned. He said, "No, you need to preach," but Kilpatrick, who had nothing left inside, insisted. Hill reluctantly agreed. No one at that dinner had any inclination that, in fifteen hours, their lives would be turned upside down in the glory of God.

It is vital to not only contemplate revival but also the types of things that become a catalyst for it. Sometimes one small act will position a church to step into their glorious destiny. Can you recognize the meaning of the calm before the storm?

> "Lord, I have heard of Your fame; I stand in awe of Your deeds, Lord. Repeat them in our day, in our time make them known; in wrath remember mercy" (Habakkuk 3:2 NIV).

14

BROWNSVILLE REVIVAL (PART TWO)

Brownsville Assembly of God

"The Christian life is not a constant high. I have my moments of deep discouragement. I have to go to God in prayer with tears in my eyes, and say, 'Oh God forgive me,' or 'Help me.' ...The will of God will not take us where the grace of God cannot sustain us."—Billy Graham

"The first thing most churches need to do is to get God to attend."—Steve Gray

"Our praying, however, needs to be pressed and pursued with an energy that never tires, a persistency which will not be denied, and a courage which never fails."—E. M. Bounds

"If I could, I would finalize the training of my soldiers by hanging them over an open hell, to see its eternal torment."—William Booth

"The man who can get believers to praying would under God, usher in the greatest revival that the world has ever known. There is no fault in God."—Leonard Ravenhill

⌇

W hile individuals prepare their hearts and earnestly pray, true revival is often unexpected. God shatters the silence with incredible works of power.

Sunday, June 18, 1995, felt like a typical day in the beach-side community of Pensacola, Florida. Vacationers were wading in the warm Gulf waters. Veterans were lined up to enter the National Naval Aviation Museum, seeing the beauty of World War II fighter planes. While vacationing families were busy having fun, the locals were sleeping in, oblivious that anything out of the ordinary was about to happen.

On this sunny Father's Day, thousands were attending church in Pensacola, but even the faithful did not see what God had in store for their community. This resort community was about to experience soul-stirring revival! A portal was about to be opened that would touch the earth.

When John Kilpatrick, the pastor of Brownsville Assembly of God, awoke, he felt exhausted. Health issues, church conflict, and the recent death of his mother weighed heavy on his heart. He wanted out. He prepared to call the lead elder to clarify that he would not be at the service and that he wanted to resign.

Before he could make the call, he imagined the face of a four-year-old from his congregation he had grown to love. This sweet little girl would often pull on his trouser leg and say, "I love you, preacher." Kilpatrick's congregation always honored a single dad with the Best Godly Single Father of the Year Award. The four-year-old's father was receiving recognition this year, and he didn't want to miss the joy on her face. Pulling his hand from the phone, his pastoral heart kept him from making the call.

Kilpatrick was glad he invited Steve Hill to preach that morning. The evangelist had ministered to the congregation several times over the years. Many knew who he was and what to expect. The pastor sensed the favor on Hill's life and knew that he was a fire-brand for the Kingdom of God. He was grateful to have someone so dependable in the pulpit during this difficult moment.

HILL BEGINS HIS MESSAGE

Kilpatrick introduced Hill, and as he stepped into the pulpit, the congregation sensed that something was different. The young evangelist shone with the glory of God and burned with a fresh passion. The people could even hear something in the tone of his voice.

After addressing the congregation, Hill had the people turn to Psalm 77:11. The text reads: "I will remember the works of the Lord; surely I will remember Your wonders of old. I will meditate also on all Your work and ponder on Your mighty deeds."

What Hill said next was prophetic:

"This may be Father's Day, but friends, the Lord is going somewhere today… We are all going to look back and say, I remember Father's Day of 1993. I remember 1994, but let me talk to you about what happened in 1995. You will say, I'll never forget that Sunday. I will never forget what happened to me on that day. We will all remember the deeds of the Lord."

For the next forty-five minutes, Hill recounted the story of the powerful work of the Spirit he encountered at Holy Trinity Anglican Church in Brompton, England. He explained to Brownsville Assembly of God that everything had changed for him. He received a fresh fire from God, and they could have it too.

Although God was moving through Hill's message, Kilpatrick was struggling. His inner pain closed him off to the work that was transpiring in the room. Hearing the evangelist's words, Kilpatrick thought, "Don't say that again, I already heard it, do not say it again." Hill later acknowledged, "Pastor John was getting ticked off, not knowing where I was going with my message."

God was stirring, but obstacles remained in the room—the greatest of which was the senior pastor. Although feeling the pushback, Hill was not dismayed. As he continued his message, the spirit of God melted hearts and removed the impediments.

THE ALTAR CALL

As he finished the sermon, Hill declared that if anyone needed a fresh encounter from the Lord, they should come forward. Around one thousand responded to his call to action.

When Hill went over to pour some anointing oil on his hands, Kilpatrick said, "My God, Steve, it's Father's Day! These people want to honor their fathers and take them out to eat. Now we are going to have to pray for all these people."

Undeterred, the evangelist jumped off the platform like a gazelle and began to lay hands on the multitudes. Hill shouted, above the thundering music, "Touch him, Jesus," "More Lord," "Fresh touch."

As Hill moved through the crowd, many were overcome with God's glory. No longer able to hold themselves up, they fell to the ground, trembling. Kilpatrick was watching what was going on and he knew that he couldn't remain on the stage. So, he got up from his chair to join in this time of ministry. The pastor shared the following recollection,

> "I decided I needed to help him pray for all these people so with slumped shoulders I walked across the platform saying to myself that I better put on my preacher face and stepped onto the steps. When I did that I had no idea that my life, this church and the world would be forever changed."

KILPATRICK TOUCHED

Something unexpected transpired as Kilpatrick got up from his seat. He felt something unusual—an inexplicable work of God. He later said it was like being swept into a swift-flowing stream of water. Kilpatrick could first sense it circling around his legs, but it increased. Many would later call it this mighty work of the Spirit the "River of God."

Other things were transpiring as God moved upon Kilpatrick and the whole church. It was like the mighty wind described in the Book of Acts. As the Spirit rumbled through the sanctuary, the "wind" sounded like a hand was rubbing across the microphone. This bizarre sound confused the media team. The camera operators checked their headsets, wondering if they were malfunctioning.

The flow of the "river" was so strong around Kilpatrick's legs that his knees buckled. One usher noticed and asked if everything was okay. The pastor told him, "No, I can't stand. Get me back on the platform." Once there, Kilpatrick grabbed a microphone and shouted over the cries and supernatural sounds,

"My God church, Get in! This is it! This is what we have been praying for! Get in! I tell you I have never felt the power of God like I feel it right now. I'm telling you this: there is power in this place! Receive it!"

People in the back rushed to the front at this invitation. As Kilpatrick stepped forward, the glory of God overwhelmed him. He fell backwards across the steps with a loud thud. Daniel K. Norris, one participant, recounted what happened,

> "The moment Pastor Kilpatrick spoke those words, the heavens above the church opened, and the Spirit of God filled the room. Whole groups of people began to be swept off their feet. From his vantage point on the stage, he saw people falling everywhere . . . He started descending the steps again, but instead collapsed hard to the floor. His head bounced on the marble floor . . . He would lie there for nearly four hours unable to move under the glory of God."

When Kilpatrick went out in the spirit, there was a collective "whoa" from the camera team that echoed through the headsets. The video director instructed them to keep filming what was happening up front. He sensed that this was something extraordinary because his pastor "would not take a courtesy dive for anyone." This had to be God.

This was not the typical response from Kilpatrick. Describing his experience, he later wrote, "When I hit the floor, it felt like I weighed one thousand pounds. I knew something supernatural was happening. God was visiting us."

Steve Hill was being touched as well as he moved through the crowd. He recalled,

> "I believe that it was a real special divine appointment . . . it was totally spontaneous . . . The Father showed up on Father's

Day... and just loved on us. And you know everybody got back to work . . . going after God, because they felt the nearness of the Lord."

The service lasted until four in the afternoon, with the shouts of hundreds of worshippers crying out for God. Pastor Kilpatrick was finally helped off the floor, still dazed by God's presence. Brenda Kilpatrick was asked if she wanted to leave for dinner and she said, "No, you go ahead, I waited too long for this and I don't want to leave it." Although some grabbed food and made it back for the service at 6:00 p.m., for many, it was like the service never ended.

In the evening service, Hill preached again, and it was wracked with more power than the morning. Kilpatrick was again slouched in his chair "out in the Spirit." Before finishing his message, the evangelist mentioned he would be back the next night if anyone wanted to attend. This powerful gathering continued until after midnight.

On Father's Day, June 18, 1995, Brownsville Assembly of God became a lightning rod of spiritual power. The Holy Spirit came in unprecedented power. What began as a powerful Sunday morning service continued for days and weeks. In fact, the fire continued to burn in Pensacola for almost six years.

THE SLEEPING PASTOR

During the first six months of the revival, the Lord was dealing with Kilpatrick. The glory continually overcame him. There were nights when he could not move and had to be carried out of the church in a wheelchair. One evening, he didn't show up at the service. His son went home and found him in bed, so overcome by the Holy Spirit that he couldn't get his socks on.

While Hill preached, he would look over and see Kilpatrick slumped in the chair. Knowing his conservative friend was so waylaid by God that he couldn't hold his head up was unexpected. He said, "This was so cool, it had to be God."

Kilpatrick's son, John Michael, invited a friend to a revival service, and the guest asked him, "Why does your dad sleep through the whole service?"

During this time, Kilpatrick was still struggling with the unusual supernatural manifestations in the services—it rubbed his religion raw. God often laid him out on the floor and gave him a fresh taste of the Holy Spirit. Bit by bit, the pastor was gaining a greater sense of freedom and joy.

THE REVIVAL EXPANDS

God was at work in Pensacola and transforming the entire landscape. Many Brownsville Assembly of God members were overwhelmed by the glory, but not all appreciated what was transpiring. Forty families left the church after the revival began. They thought that the falling and shaking were out of order.

While some disliked what was occurring, Hill was elated. He sat under Leonard Ravenhill and heard the accounts of the older awakenings in America. Where others were unsure, he was ready to go. Hill canceled everything on his calendar and committed to remain in Pensacola as long as the revival continued. He moved his wife and children to the Florida panhandle to stand alongside him.

Although Hill was an evangelist, the revival initially focused on Brownsville Assembly of God members. Many stayed and prayed until the early morning. Finally stumbling out of the sanctuary at 1:00 or 2:00 in the morning, many said, "See ya'll later today." Some had to be helped to their cars. Many sat behind the wheel, motionless, for hours—under the influence of the Spirit.

Word spread about what was happening, and crowds of people arrived in Pensacola. First, it was the hungry from nearby communities, but later individuals from faraway places made their way to Brownsville Assembly of God.

John Kilpatrick and the youth pastor, Richard Crisco, were in the parking lot as a large bus from South Carolina parked. Over fifty hungry people came off the greyhound, saying, "This is where God is." Crisco couldn't believe it. With shock in his voice, he said, "You mean you came from South Carolina?" This was the first of thousands of busloads from around the United States. Soon, hundreds were flying in from overseas. The building was packed with hungry souls.

Trying to ensure they'd get a seat in the main sanctuary, people arrived as early as five o'clock in the morning. They brought lawn chairs and ice chests. Some set up large umbrellas and canvas pavilions to shelter their awaiting families from the scorching sun. All over the church grounds, you would hear worship music pumping from boomboxes.

It was not rare to see 1,500 people waiting for the 7:00 pm service. Lines stretched across the parking lot, out the gate, and down the street—past the bingo hall landmark. Hundreds couldn't wait to get in and receive a fresh touch from God.

The revival participants would later share things like the following:

> "We've come to see the glory of God . . . you can feel His presence . . . His presence is awesome."

> "God comes in like the tide of the ocean and you can feel it."

> "We came because we wanted to be where God was."

> "I had been addicted to alcohol, pain medication and anti-depressants... I even had problems with cocaine and crack... since coming to this revival God has delivered me from them all . . . I feel such peace inside."

The revival drew diverse ages, races and socioeconomic conditions. Pastor Kilpatrick reported:

> "Corporate businessmen in expensive suits kneel and weep uncontrollably as they repent of secret sins. Drug addicts and prostitutes fall to the floor on their faces beside them, to lie prostrate before God as they confess Jesus as Lord for the first time in their lives. Reserved elderly women and weary young mothers dance unashamedly before the Lord with joy. They have been forgiven. Young children see an incredible vision of Jesus, their faces a picture of divine delight framed by slender arms lifted heavenward."

To accommodate crowds, they held services Wednesday through Sunday. Later, Kilpatrick and his team added an afternoon training for pastors and a prayer meeting. Thousands were gathering most nights through the week, desperate to have a deeper encounter with the Lord.

At the start of the services, Lindell Cooley led the worship, bringing powerful new intercessory expressions that took the congregants into the glorious presence of the Lord.

Steve Hill filled the pulpit at most Brownsville Assembly of God revival services. He typically emphasized biblical messages of sin, repentance, and salvation. As Hill finished his sermons, hundreds ran to the altar to "get right with God." As Charity James sang the soul-shaking "Mercy Seat," people fell to their knees.

Ministry teams moved through the crowd to pray for needs. As they "released the power of God," many trembled and fell to the ground. People were not only experiencing salvation but also signs and wonders. Steve Hill noted, "We're seeing miraculous healings, cancerous tumors disappear and drug addicts are immediately delivered."

Besides tens of thousands giving their lives to Jesus, the

revival was transforming the city. The Pensacola mayor and sheriff visited the revival many times and reported the city's drop in crime. The move of God was making a tangible impact on the community.

With all the growing attention, the news media descended upon the Florida panhandle. *The New York Times, Washington Post, PBS, CNN, CBS, NBC, ABC,* and others published reports, bringing even more recognition to what was transpiring in Pensacola.

Over the next five years, close to five million people traveled to take part in the Brownsville Revival. This glorious stirring of God was affecting people around the nation. The fervor continued to escalate.

Kilpatrick, Hill, and Cooley organized revival crusades in Anaheim, Dallas, St. Louis, Toledo, Birmingham, and other cities. They called this effort "Awake America," and multitudes were touched with the glory of God in these gatherings.

They also launched the Brownsville Revival School of Ministry under the oversight of Michael Brown. Just two years in, one thousand students were enrolled and many of the alumni were doing missionary work in 122 nations.

NEW WINE IN OLD WINESKINS

God was at work in Pensacola, but some of the underlying cracks were showing. It is hard for a newer revival to burn bright in an older denomination. As Jesus said, "No one puts new wine into old wineskins" (Matthew 9:17).

Throughout the revival, denominational tensions intensified. Many of the Assemblies of God officials were uncomfortable with the unusual manifestations. Some criticized the approach to finances and the curriculum at the Brownsville Revival School of Ministry.

Bureaucrats kept making much of the friction points,

although most were inconsequential. But when one keeps picking at a scab, it causes inflammation. The criticism took its toll.

In 2001, because of denominational pressures, there was a split between the leadership of the church and overseers of the Brownsville Revival School of Ministry. In many ways, this split marked the beginning of the end of the revival.

It was difficult for the revival leaders to pivot. The pre-existing systems were not designed to be disrupted. After some of the rising tensions, Steve Hill left to launch a new church in Dallas, Texas. Not long afterward, worship leader Lindell Cooley left, founding a church in Franklin, Tennessee. Finally, Pastor Kilpatrick resigned from Brownsville Assembly of God to establish the Church of His Presence in Daphne, Alabama.

Although these men continued to carry the fire of revival, very little of that anointing remained in Pensacola, Florida. The greatest Pentecostal Revival in a generation quietly passed from the scene.

SHAPING A NEW REVIVAL CONSCIOUSNESS

God always has a way to stir the hearts of his people. He comes in unexpected ways. The Brownsville Revival transformed Pentecostal-Charismatic Christianity. It shaped a new revival consciousness that opened the door to deeper works of the Spirit in the twenty-first century.

Vinson Synan, the late Pentecostal historian and Dean of Regent University School of Divinity, shared the following observations about the Pensacola Outpouring:

> "The emphasis on conversion and people weeping over their
> conviction of sin seems to be a revival in the tradition of
> American native revivals dating back to Jonathan Edwards.
> There is heavy preaching on sin, repentance, conversion, and

holiness and a lot more of weeping and wailing over sin, then there are the so-called exotic manifestations."

Synan was reminding his multi-generational, Spirit-filled audience that the Brownsville Revival was merely a continuation of the older Pentecostal traditions.

Amid lethargy and darkness, God will always come and revive his people. Moreover, the embers of one generation's revival often stir the flames of later era. Revive us once again, Lord!

"And the Lord, whom you seek, will suddenly come to His temple" (Malachi 3:1).

15

THE SMITHTON OUTPOURING

The Old Smithton Meetinghouse

"These wounds are meant to purchase me. These drops of blood were shed to obtain me. I am not my own today. I belong to another. I have been bought with a price. And I will live every minute of every day so that the Great Purchaser of my soul will receive the full reward of His suffering."—Count Nikolaus Ludwig Von Zinzendorf

"Will You not revive us again, that Your people may rejoice in You."—Sons of Korah (Psalm 85:6)

"When is revival needed? When carelessness and unconcern keep the people asleep."—Billy Sunday

"Prayer is the burden of revival; repentance is the breakthrough of revival; evangelism is the blessing of revival; holiness is the bounty of revival."—Steve Camp

"The first step [for revival] is a deep repentance, a breaking down of the heart, getting down into the dust before God, with deep humility, and a forsaking of sin."—Charles G. Finney

⁓

As a warm breeze rustled through the old trees, they were standing at attention—like sentinels—keeping watch over a hamlet in the heartland of America. The mournful wail of a Union Pacific locomotive rumbling, along with a cacophony of insects, added ambience to this late summer evening.

Excited voices emanating from the downtown playground interrupted this picturesque scene of small-town America. The incredible move of God that they had just encountered filled this small group with awe and wonder.

This group traveled across five states to visit a town not even on most maps. They wanted to find out if the stories were true. Did God, in all His glory and greatness, visit a small church in the middle of nowhere?

These out-of-towners discussed what transpired when they entered the building and felt the weight of glory. God's presence hovered over the room, bending many at the waist. They witnessed the ensuing shaking, falling, cries of joy, and tears of repentance. The heavenly presence that moved around the sanctuary felt like a warm summer breeze.

As the travelers spoke, each knew they had encountered God. Overwhelmed by His presence and consumed by His love, they would never be the same again.

For three and a half years, in the late 1990s, a quarter-of-a-million traveled to this small town to encounter the presence and power of God. They considered it the third most significant North American revival—joining the Toronto Blessing and the Brownsville Revival as a key pilgrimage spot.

Pat Robertson visited the midwestern revival and gave the following eyewitness account:

> "From the time you step into the service, you see the hunger the people have for God's glory. The desire and expectation crescendos during worship into the very presence and glory of God filling the room... Bringing the people to their knees, weeping. As His glory moves, people are healed, set free and changed."

Christianity Today magazine called this move of God, "The Cornfield Revival." Some Asian pastors traveling to the heartland called it, "The Revival from Nowhere," but most called it, "The Smithton Outpouring."

SMITHTON, MISSOURI, A TINY HAMLET

Smithton Missouri, population 532, was an unlikely locale for anything notable to happen—let alone an internationally recognized move of God. The residents were quiet and reserved, wanting to separate themselves from the pace of city life. Many wanted to be isolated—closed off from the rest of the world.

The attitude of this town was plain to most anyone who entered its borders. It had no traffic light, gas station, or restaurant. For several years, there wasn't even a Coke machine. Outsiders couldn't stay there. The nearest lodging was nine miles away. Driving down gravel roads, one saw dilapidated farmhouses, lots with tractors and farm implements, and the cornfields swaying back and forth in the wind. Smithton was so small and unassuming that it was absent from most maps.

This quiet community became a home for Steve and Kathy Gray in January 1979. After a tornado in nearby Sedalia had decimated their duplex, they were looking for a new home to rest. The three-bedroom house they found in Smithton seemed to fit the bill. But the furthest thing from Steve's mind was being a pastor in this tiny hamlet.

DENIED CALLINGS

After Steve Gray's father died in 1968, he took on a "desperado" persona, getting entangled in fights and growing long hair. Along with other trappings of the hippie lifestyle, he carried a set of brass knuckles in his pocket. He didn't look for fights, but was prepared for them when they came.

While still in High School, Gray and his brother performed in a rock-n-roll band called "The Magnolia Opera Company." They performed in bars, and once for the Kansas City Mafia. Gray's swashbuckling, shoot from the hip attitude drew many to him and took him on many adventures.

However, this young man's wild, rock-n-roll persona was a far cry from where he had journeyed. As a young boy, God struck his heart after a Sunday morning service at the Nazarene Church in Hays, Kansas. His mother and father found him lying at the altar alone, crying out to the Lord. When he arose, he said, "I have been called to preach." Although Gray moved further from God, he still felt pieces of that moment. Amid depravity, the pull of the Lord continued.

After graduating from High School, Gray stumbled his way

into Central Missouri University in Warrensburg. Jim Goll, and others in the burgeoning Jesus Movement, targeted Gray in their evangelistic pursuits. One knocked on his dorm door and asked, "If you were to die tonight, do you know where you would go?" Gray, with a cigarette hanging out of his mouth, smugly asked, "What if I don't die tonight?" The young evangelist didn't know what to say.

Jim Goll later said, "Steve Gray was number one on my prayer hit list." Believers at Central Missouri thought the singer was godless, but they didn't see what God was doing in his heart. Gray periodically attended church services. Although they were formal and dry, he would weep. God was at work in this troubled young man.

Gray met a young woman named Katy Moffatt through the "One and Only Singers," a performance group from the college. She was attracted to his bad boy image and he was drawn to her stability. After dating several months, he told her he had nothing to offer, but if she married him, she would "never have a dull moment in her life."

Steve and Kathy married in early 1975 because of a teaching offer—as husband and wife—in the Ludlow school district in Northern Missouri. The new responsibilities tamed Gray to some degree, but he still liked to drink and run with his raucous buddies. Kathy was frustrated with the different roads they were traveling. If things didn't change, they were headed for disaster.

SAVED AND EMPOWERED

On July 20, 1975, mere months into their marriage, the two contemplated divorce. Conflict was high and their differing approaches to life didn't mesh very well. But before calling it quits, the two visited Steve's mother, Jeanne, in Sedalia. This would prove to be a divine appointment.

Over the previous year, Jeanne had been swept up in the

Charismatic Renewal. Although still active at the Wesley United Methodist Church, she attended outside prayer meetings and Bible studies. As the Lord stirred her heart, she prayed for the salvation of her family. She was particularly concerned about Steve.

Steve didn't know what to think about his mom's new found faith. Although he felt she had gone off the deep end, something about her fervency drew him in.

Steve also noticed his sister, Nancy. The last time he saw her, she had sunken eyes and her hair was falling out. Now, he witnessed a bright-eyed woman with a thick blonde hair. Nancy's obvious changes affected him in ways that he didn't expect.

Jeanne talked to Steve and Kathy about the grace of Jesus and the baptism in the Holy Spirit. She explained, with Nancy by her side, how they were filled with the love of God. As this hurting couple listened, a longing arose.

When Jeanne asked if they'd like to have the same experiences that people in the Bible had, they agreed. God had been working on Steve for a long time, but he had been fighting the pull. Rock-n-roll and worldliness had him entangled. But God was in pursuit of this broken young man.

Both Steve and Kathy submitted to the wooing of the Holy Spirit. They fell to their knees and cried out to God. Within moments, they were saved and Spirit-baptized. Steve, encountering the power of God, sang in unknown tongues.

On the living room floor, a couple was restored and melded together to take part in an amazing mission. They said, "yes," to an adventure that would change the lives of thousands around the world.

MINISTRY BEGINS

After a brief time of training and preparation, the Grays launched an itinerate ministry—preaching and singing around the United

States. Steve's mother, his siblings, and their spouses joined them. They called themselves Jubilation.

For almost seven years, the family traveled on a greyhound bus, ministering in any venue that would receive them. Along the way, Gray became a prolific song writer—penning a top-ten gospel hit, "Promises."

Yet, the wear and tear of traveling took its toll. Some of the family didn't want to continue. Gray, himself, sensed that God was up to something new.

One night in 1983, while in prayer, Steve heard the Lord say that revival was coming to local churches in America. He didn't want to miss this; so he told Kathy to cancel their future engagements. They were going to hide away and see what God was up to.

The Grays settled in the town of Smithton, Missouri. Steve took an associate pastor position in a Pentecostal church in Sedalia, and Kathy began teaching again. They didn't know what was next but were excited about the possibilities of the future.

In the midst of prayerful searching, they received an unexpected offer to serve in a large church in a suburb of Chicago. The pastor was contemplating retirement and wanted Gray to be raised up to lead the church. This was a growing congregation with eight hundred members. The offer also came with a generous salary and benefits package.

This appeared to be exactly what God was directing them toward. They joyfully accepted this offer and began to look for a house in northern Illinois.

"A man's heart plans his way, but the Lord directs his steps." (Proverbs 16:9)

THE OLD MEETINGHOUSE

After five years of living in Smithton, the Grays had no intention of establishing a ministry there. They didn't know much about the community; they just slept there. But there was an old building on the other side of town with a rich history.

This vacant building was constructed with large wooden pegs in 1859. This quaint, paneled meetinghouse looked like something on a Currier and Ives print.

Disciples of Barton Stone, the revivalist who sparked the Cane Ridge Camp meeting, originally constructed it in Farmer's City. These people called themselves, "Christians"—wanting to restore New Testament Christianity in America. (Interestingly, a founder of the Smithton Methodist Church was a participant in the Cane Ridge Revival).

Over time, Farmer City dried up and became a ghost town. The remaining residents moved and brought their meeting house to Smithton, a few miles away. In 1873, the building was cut into quarters and moved by oxen to 200 South Chestnut Avenue, where it was put back together and became a sanctuary for several generations of believers. However, after a century of services, the doors were closed in 1980 and the building fell into disrepair.

RAISE THE DEAD

A family in Smithton approached Steve and Kathy; asking them to restart a church in the old meetinghouse. They weren't interested in the Gray's ministry, but they didn't want this old landmark to be torn down.

To Steve, this didn't seem like a good opportunity. The exterior paint was peeling and everything was in need of repair. Inside, the timeworn pews left brown marks on people's clothes. The only occupants of the building over the last few years were rats and birds, and their decaying bodies were scattered throughout.

When one walked through the creaky door of this edifice, the noxious smells were overwhelming. If all of this was not bad enough, there were no remaining members and little prospect of growth in this five-hundred person town.

Steve was kind, but rebuffed their requests. He made it clear that his family was making preparations to relocate to Chicago. He didn't see the tiny town of Smithton as his next ministry assignment. As graciously as possible, he said, "I don't know what all happened, but there was probably a good reason for that church to be closed."

Weeks later, they came to him again with the offer. Gray basically gave the same response. This wasn't something he wanted to do. A growing church was waiting for him in Chicago.

Shockingly, Gray was approached a third time. They were willing to do anything, and relinquish everything, if he would only take over the meetinghouse. Gray still had no intention of deviating from his plans, but he assured them that he would pray about it.

In the natural, there was no question about which one was the better opportunity. In the suburbs of Chicago, they were going to be well-paid pastors—positioned to take over the congregation. Kathy was going to teach in their private school. In addition, they already picked out a spacious brick house.

Remaining in Smithton, he would have to restart a church in a building built before the Civil War. There were no members, and they were living in a low population area. Essentially, there was no real prospect for income. Most would say that the decision was clear. That's certainly what Gray thought.

Promising he would pray about the matter, Gray half-heartedly took it before the Lord. He gave his word, but didn't think there was any question about his assignment. He prayed,

"Lord, I have this wonderful offer in Chicago. It's a big church offering me a good salary, benefits, and endless opportunities. Now, they are talking to me about this old run down building in Smithton. They want me to pastor a church with no congregation. Everything is dead. What would you do?"

Amid the intercession, Gray heard a shocking response from the Lord. It was like a voice audibly said, "I'll tell you what I would do—I would raise the dead!" As soon as Gray heard this, he thought, "Oh No!"

It's not that Gray couldn't go to Chicago. God would have blessed that decision, but if he really wanted to walk in the favor of the Lord, he needed to be willing to go into the wilderness.

So, Steve and Kathy inherited an old, white clapboard building with dead birds and vermin. There was no congregation and no money. They were going to have to start out with nothing.

THE BEGINNING OF SMITHTON COMMUNITY CHURCH

Steve and Kathy did their best to clean up the building and get things ready for the first service. On Thursday, April 19, 1984, they placed a sign in the yard that said, "Church Service Tonight," and eleven people joined them. The next week a few more showed up, and Smithton Community Church finally launched a Sunday morning service in May.

Vision was riding high and Gray preached to two dozen people like he was preaching to thousands. He poured out his heart, telling them that revival was coming. This was a deeply felt message that he never let up on.

Gray would stand behind the pulpit in this white paneled meetinghouse and read stirring accounts of the old revivals. He would recount tales from the Great Awakening, Cane Ridge, and

Prayer Revival of 1857-1858. When he spoke, the people felt like they were experiencing—first hand—the moves of God from prior centuries.

Stirred with a vision for revival, Gray told his small audience that long lines of people would one day be waiting to get inside their church. He said, "Imagine people waiting outside the front door of Smithton Community Church for a fresh touch of God. Can you see that?" Most of the people couldn't imagine that happening in their tiny town, but Gray was persuaded that God was going to do something incredible.

PRAYING FOR REVIVAL

In the 1980s and early 90s, the American church was full of lukewarm, half-hearted religion. Preachers were preaching dead sermons to dead congregations. But during this era, Gray became a voice of fresh air. He preached soul-stirring messages that quickened the hearts of many. Little by little, the church grew.

Gray continued to talk about moves of God, but as the years continued, he wondered if it was really going to happen in the wilderness of Missouri. What would it look like for there to be a revival in his church? These kinds of thoughts kept him awake at night.

In the 1990s, Gray began hearing rumors of revival in various places. One of the first that caught his attention was the fourteen-week Rodney Howard-Browne stirring in Lakeland, Florida. In 1993, the Grays visited one of his overflow services in St. Louis, Missouri, and were intrigued by what they saw. At the time, Gray wasn't sure if it was a genuine revival, but God was moving the puzzle pieces around. One thing was obvious, American Christianity was missing something vital.

The Grays began hearing about outpourings of the Holy Spirit in Toronto, England, Argentina, and Pensacola. It felt like good things were happening everywhere but Smithton, Missouri.

Privately, Gray wondered what was wrong with Smithton Community Church and its tired pastor. What did they need to do to be ready for the future? He had been preaching revival for over a decade and was concerned that his church might be left behind in the next move of God.

To position the church for revival, Gray launched a prayer meeting every Tuesday night. He hoped that his congregation would press into the throne of heaven, but found that they struggled with intercession. Most couldn't pray over thirty-seconds without running out of steam.

Instead of shouting their prayers and putting energy into it, they whispered a few lines and trailed off. Most wanted to leave after a few minutes of interceding.

Gray took it upon himself to train the people in prayer. He instructed them to join their voices and focus on one or two needs. It was important that the people learn to pray for unity and the moving of the Spirit. What lasted only fifteen minutes progressively developed and expanded. Finally, the congregation prayed for an hour or more.

Every Tuesday night for two years, Smithton Community Church stormed the throne of grace. The underlying goal was for God's presence to consume them. This revival-focused service was soon the most sought out each week. Things were beginning to change in the church, but the move of God still felt out of reach. This weighed on Gray. He said,

> "I began to hear things in the world, revivals, little fires springing up. Yet it was not happening in my place. I began to feel stuck in this small town . . . After years of sitting, hoping and dreaming you start moving in the other direction. You think that this is not going to happen."

Gray had been preaching and preparing his people for revival for years, but it still wasn't manifest. Why was this? If God sent revival to other places, why did he seem to withhold it on Smithton? The congregation had been praying for it and standing for it—but where is it? Some asked, "Did we do something wrong? Are we too small?"

Gray reflected on this, writing:

> "It was difficult preaching about a coming revival to a handful of people in the early years of Smithton Community Church. Revival did not come suddenly as I thought it would. We yearned and prayed and cheered and sang for it, but it did not come... I preached as though there were thousands in attendance... I preached so many sermons in that little church that I could walk forward, backward and up and down the steps with my eyes closed."

Besides the lackluster spiritual growth in the church, Gray was dealing with other disappointments. His beloved mother passed away. He was also dealing with conflicts with a couple families in the church. In addition, his daughter, who was a major part of his life, was engaged to be married. Gray felt like things were slipping out of his grip.

He had gone to the well for spiritual stamina many times, and it felt like it was running dry. His dream of God moving mightily through him and his church was withering, and he knew it.

As things were growing difficult, Gray's sister approached him and gave him a warning from the Lord:

> "Steve would be betrayed by some people that he cared deeply for... I felt that if I didn't warn him, I would regret it for the rest of my life. So I went to him and told him he needed to be prepared for this."

What Diana revealed from the Lord challenged Gray. He knew that he was dealing with a few conflicts, but he didn't expect it to escalate to this level. He sensed that his sister's words were accurate, but this revelation still crushed him. Gray later acknowledged, "It broke my heart. My heart just collapsed. The life went out of me."

After years of pouring out their lives for the people, some people treacherously turned against the Grays. They not only stirred up trouble in the church, they tried to get others to turn against the ministry.

Gray had enough. He was hurt, tired, and overwhelmed. He didn't feel like he could continue as the pastor of this flock. Many times people had betrayed him, but this time was different. He felt the weight of the loss.

Gray didn't know what to do, but what he wanted was to get away where no one knew him. Maybe he could go on an extended mission trip to the Philippines or run away to a remote island. He tearfully told Kathy that he thought God was through with him. The next moves were unclear, but he couldn't imagine staying on at Smithton Community Church. He had reached the end of the line and he didn't want to hurt anymore.

NOTHING LEFT BUT FAITH

On Sunday, March 10, 1996, Gray stood before Smithton Community Church to preach his last sermon before leaving town. In this message, he spoke about the woman with the issue of blood. He explained how she spent all she had and was no better. Without being overt, he let them know he was like that woman. He had poured out his life for revival and gave all he had for that congregation, and now he was coming up short.

The congregation was waiting for the sermon to shift into the grace-filled solution, but Gray did not provide it. One member later said, "I knew Pastor Steve was hurt by the way he preached that message. I had never heard him preach a sermon without hope." After he finished speaking that morning, he walked out the door and left.

Gray was looking for a place to get away to. When he heard about a revival breaking out at the Brownsville Assembly of God Church in Pensacola, Florida, that seemed like the perfect place to go. Kathy pleaded with him to go there. She said, "Our church would understand you going somewhere to check out a revival." Gray didn't care where he went, he just needed to get away from Smithton.

This broken man got into his car and drove twenty hours to Pensacola, Florida. He said: "I drove away hopelessly . . . I didn't even know why I was going there . . . I was not after revival. I was after survival."

IT'S COMING, I KNOW IT'S COMING

While Gray was in Florida, Smithton Community Church went through intense soul-searching, too. Kathy was guiding and teaching the people about the deeper works of the Holy Spirit. She was working to hold the congregation together as their pastor sought God.

In one service, Kathy told the congregation that Steve called and told her he "just experienced the best church service ever." She thought this would encourage the people, but it broke their hearts. An elder ran to the microphone, with a holy jealousy, declaring,

> "If we don't have the true presence of God in our church, we might as well shut the place down… God what's wrong with us? Why does revival come to others and not us? Why would our pastor have to travel a thousand miles and go to a different church to experience the best service he has ever been to? Why are we shamed that our pastor must go somewhere else to find revival? God help us!"

With these heartfelt words, men rushed the altar and fell on their faces—weeping and crying out for God's mercy. Things were breaking at Smithton Community Church and God was preparing them for what was next.

On Wednesday, March 20, the members of the church gathered again and God was stirring their hearts. The people were praying and repenting. God was changing the landscape of the congregation. On that night, they brought some children up front and they prophesied. They spoke about the goodness and the holiness of God falling upon the church. One five-year-old girl, in her father's arms, pointed her finger to the sky and said, "It's coming, it's coming! I know it's coming!"

I WANT YOU TO HAVE A REVIVAL

In Florida, Gray would only leave his room to go to revival services in the evening. During the day, he rarely ate or left his bed. Housekeeping knocked on the door and he'd shout, "Go away!" They thought he was insane. Gray spent all day in fasting, prayer, and biblical study.

Not wanting to be a nuisance to the other guests, he stuffed his face into a pillow as he cried out to God. He hoped his prayers were muffled, but the hotel staff thought he was a deranged man. Their attitude about Gray is hilarious because a Star Trek convention was being held nearby and people were walking around the halls with pointed ears, green faces, and strange alien outfits. Who was the crazy man?

Gray prayed outrageous prayers. He didn't know it, but God already answered his pleas. As the Psalmist proclaims, "This poor man cried out, and the Lord heard him and saved him out of all his troubles" (Psalm 34:6).

Gray had been attending the revival services at Brownsville Assembly of God and one night, God spoke to him. This was not the message that he expected to receive. The Lord said, "I want you to have a revival." He thought that was ridiculous and brushed it off. The next night he heard it again, "I want you to have a revival."

Gray thought that this was the most absurd thing that he ever heard. He thought, "How could I, with my failings and needs, have a revival?" This seemed too far-fetched. Then the Lord clarified some things to him. He said, "I didn't tell you to be a revival, I told you to have a revival."

This explanation impacted Gray. He realized he could be a "host" for a revival and allow the Lord to do the work. If he didn't have to carry it, he could come alongside and hold the door open. That was within his capability. Knowing that God could move in spite of him changed everything for Gray. He had a willing heart and the faith to say, "Yes!"

Gray called Kathy and told her, "Today, my hope returned." For the first time in weeks, she sensed her husband was coming back. The dark night was almost over.

After checking out of the motel, Gray headed home. He still felt a little burnt out and wasn't sure he still wanted to pastor in Smithton. He had a lot of questions and didn't know what to expect when he made it home. Would God do something extraordinary or not? He didn't know what he would face when he walked through the door of that sanctuary.

THE REVIVAL SPARKS

On the evening of March 24, 1996, Gray was scheduled to return to Smithton Community Church, but he was running late. The congregation was excited about their pastor's return. Many hoped that he had received a fresh touch from God and would continue to guide them forward. Most did not understand the challenges their pastor walked through, but they loved him and were excited to see him.

When the service began at 6:00 p.m., Gray still had not

arrived and Kathy was restless. Eric Nuzum Thomason was leading worship at the church, and led the people in a rousing praise number, "Who is Like the Lord." The people were clapping and singing, but whole room was contemplating the entrance of their pastor. Kathy kept looking at her watch and at the door, wondering when her husband was going to arrive.

Gray pulled up into the parking lot, took a deep breath and entered the sanctuary. As he pushed open the door, he wondered what he was going to encounter. Everything was on the line as he came into the room.

Kathy had looked down at her watch one last time before the door opened and it said: 6:12. She saw her husband sheepishly come into the room. He made a few steps toward her to embrace her and then everything was disrupted.

After a few steps, the "lightenings of God" unexpectedly struck Steve Gray. Surges of power burst through his body, and he suddenly erupted with energy. Dead weights fell off and he was overwhelmed with joy. One who was normally calm and collected began jumping, twirling, and shouting with total abandon. It was quite a sight to behold.

Kathy Gray reminisced about this moment, declaring,

> "I saw the hand of God, the lightening of God strike my
> husband. In an instant everything lifted off of him; the years of
> hurt and frustration, the years of disappointment in himself, life
> returned!"

Steve Dailey, sitting on the second row with his family, also remembers this moment, writing,

> "I watched Pastor Steve as he entered the door and walked
> toward Pastor Kathy to give her a hug. After about eight steps,
> as I watched, he was lifted up into the air. There was no
> crouching down like you do when you plan a jump. He was

standing straight and suddenly was lifted off the floor and began twirling and jumping and shouting. Pastor Steve never twirled, jumped or shouted before."

Dailey's wife, Diane, made it to the service late that night and was seated in the back row. She also took a moment to reflect on that momentous night: "I was sitting on the back row and as I watched Pastor Steve go twirling into the air, a strong wave began rolling over the people from the front to the back."

As Diane mentioned, the fervor that came upon Gray passed through him and fanned out through the entire congregation. She noticed that when this overwhelming power "reached the back, the entire church kicked off their shoes and ran toward the front and began jumping and twirling and shouting." With a powerful burst of freedom, the whole church danced alongside their pastor.

Gray was so overcome by the Holy Spirit that he could barely speak. His body trembled and shook. It was not common for him to not know what to do. But this was the most free he had ever felt and he wanted to melt into Jesus. Gray thought, "Is this really happening?"

Describing what happened next, Gray said, "I offered to pray for people. Although I didn't lay hands on anyone, people started collapsing and crying. I was awestruck." The presence of God increased to a level never previously experienced in the congregation. One congregant remarked,

"Many fell to the ground, which had not really happened before at Smithton Community Church . . . many were struck by the power of God . . . falling, and crying . . . No one wanted to leave... people were lying in each other's arms crying . . . We were hit with a great sense of unity."

Daniel Gray was awestruck like the rest of the congregation that night. He shared the following reflection:

"God blew the doors off the little church and wiped out the membership's traditional Charismatic mind-set in the river of power and energy . . . the church was literally jumping. The whole congregation was jumping up and down to the powerful praise that had burst forth . . . people were collapsing to the floor as if cut down by some machine gun . . . my whole family was there . . . sisters, brothers-in-law, nieces, nephews and kids moving together in the river. It was very powerful!"

It was a night of chaos orchestrated by the Holy Spirit. God turned everything upside down. Sad people were suddenly filled with unspeakable joy. The shouts of y reserved Midwestern families could be heard across great distances through the clapboard walls of the old meeting house. Ron McGatlin observes,

"Pastor Steve, nor Kathy, nor anyone else… knew what to do or what to expect next… yet everyone knew that, for the first time, they felt really alive and more excited than ever. They had finally broken through the invisible wall. It was as if they had been supercharged with energy from heaven as they were plunged into the heavenly fire of God."

All who were present were so consumed with the Lord's presence that no one wanted to leave. They remained late into the night. Scott and Lisa Renfrow, children's ministry leaders, noticed that when the parents came to pick up their kids, they had a dazed look. Scott heard one of them say, "I'm coming back tomorrow night at 7pm." Scott said, "What's going on? This has to be something of God."

At the end of that long evening, Pastor Steve stood before the people and said, "I'm coming back tomorrow night and pray. If you want to come, you can." That night the glory of God broke through the doors of an old white paneled meeting house and fulfilled a twelve-year-old promise.

COMING BACK

The entire congregation was reeling from what had happened on Sunday and couldn't wait to get back the following night. A few had missed previous night and wanted to make sure they were in the room on Monday. Some wondered if the fire would still burn, but as the people entered, they could feel the tangible presence of the Holy Spirit. One young girl recounted:

> "The following night . . . the lights were dim. I remember going through the door and seeing my pastor, lying flat on the floor with tears streaming down his face. This was the first I had ever seen him like that . . . this was more than jumping... and shouting. This was deep and very serious . . . there were many others who were doing the exact same thing . . . praying quietly while others were shouting at the top of their lungs . . . Pastor Steve later told us that he would be there the next evening and everyone came again."

Night after night the congregation come back and basked in the glorious presence of God. People were crying out for Jesus and repenting of their hardheartedness. Things were being shaken off the people. Kathy Gray proclaimed, "I believe this is the prelude to something great, something big. This is the rumblings of revival."

In the first few weeks, church members were purified for a work that they did not yet anticipate. Many times, God prepares people for something greater. Across the sanctuary, hearts were melted and reformed. No one was exempt. One member recalled,

"I needed Him to come and break through the hardness. If He
didn't, I was going to die. I was sick of being so hard. It took a
few weeks, but the hardness cracked and broke . . . I started
repenting and crying for Him and life came in."

God had already begun working on Gray, turning his heart
and birthing a new message, but the Lord also began a work with
his wife, Kathy. Over the years, she had let frustration and
disappointment gain a foothold. It had affected their lives in
many ways. But in the intensity of revival, wretched things are
exposed and driven from people's lives. In one meeting, the Holy
Spirit came down and ripped out ugly things in Kathy's heart.
She laughed and rejoiced, experiencing freedom like she had
never experienced before.

In the aftermath, Steve and Kathy became an explosive ministry
duo—boldly preaching and praying alongside each other. One
observer said the two were like "lightning bolts flying across the
room." When either of them prayed for people, it was like a
someone stuck their finger into an electric socket and was jolted and
shook to the floor. At the end of the revival services, people would
run over the top of each other to get down to the front to receive
prayer from the Grays or other anointed members of the team.

Lisa Renfrow remembered an early moment in the revival
when Pastor Steve prayed for her. She wrote,

"I felt a weightiness, but most of all I felt an intense heat, a fiery
feeling that started at the top of my head and it consumed my
whole being to the soles of my feet. The intensity was so
profound that I could no longer stand, so I fell to my knees and
cried and cried. This was my first experience with the tangible
presence of God."

After the events of March 24, this small congregation was

ushered into an unprecedented realm of glory. In many services, the atmosphere of the building was tangibly thick with the presence of Jesus. It was a realm where miracles became common occurrences.

In this environment, the services would continue until one in the morning, and sleep didn't seem all that relevant. In these wonderful times of gathering, marvelous experiences captivated everyone who came into the room. No one could stand without shaking or falling to their knees

Phenomenal miracles took place. Dramatic healings transpired over the first weeks and reoccurred later. Several visitors with migraine headaches felt weightiness lift off their heads as they received prayer. One member's neighbor had a fatal blood disease. They came to meetings and experienced total healing.

In one service, Gray told those assembled that an "open heaven is above you." Individuals in that service described it as if a huge fireball was pulsating over their head. As God moved through the building, people felt weightless, and some were thrown several feet across the room.

Some church members were concerned the fire would go out. Other moves of God had fizzled out quickly. Gray and his congregants didn't want the same fate to happen to their church. Some members saw themselves as the "keepers of the flame" and were willing to do anything to keep the altar burning. They cited a passage from Leviticus:

"The fire on the altar must be kept burning; it must not go out. Every morning the priest is to add firewood and arrange the burnt offering on the fire and burn the fat of the fellowship offerings on it" (Leviticus 6:12).

Yet, as the revival continued to burn, they realized that it was resilient—if they remained unified and committed to interceding together.

One of Gray's most vital teachings during this era of the outpouring was on the "Power of All." This sermon focused on the significance of the group. What believers could do together was greater than what they could do alone. There are several biblical examples of this. During the time of Joshua, all of God's people marched around Jericho and shouted—then the wall came down. On the Day of Pentecost, in the second chapter of Acts, the believers were all in one accord and the fire of the Spirit fell. When believers prayerfully stood together and moved in unison, nothing could stop them. These were principles that could keep the fire burning.

ARE THE RUMORS TRUE?

In the revival's first month, news spread quickly. People from the area were saying, "Do you really think God is doing something in Smithton?" This wasn't the kind of place most would pick for a move of God, but that became part of the mystique. God truly had to be at work when it was in such an out-of-the-way place.

The first visitors to the revival were from the local Methodist Church. These hesitant people sauntered into the building and took up a whole pew near the back. As Gray and some members prayed for them, the fire of God fell mightily. When some of the congregants saw the Methodists trembling and crying on the floor, they knew that something marvelous was happening. One member said, "These people had never been around the moving of the Holy Spirit, and they didn't believe in all the stuff we believe. But they got touched. This just goes to show you that it's God."

Others came and were also overcome in the presence of God. One Pentecostal deacon from nearby Sedalia visited and was brought to his knees in the glory. He later said, "I wasn't sure if the rumors were true, but God is moving in that little place in the cornfields."

OUR LIVES FOR HIS LIFE

Gray had a lot of preconceived ideas about what the revival was going to be like, but it turned out to be different. After being at the services at the Brownsville Revival, he thought that Smithton Community Church might emulate their approach.

In the first few weeks, they sent out evangelism teams and had extended calls for salvation during services, but these efforts yielded little fruit. Gray realized that God had given his congregation a different mandate. Smithton Community Church was being brought to the forefront to reaffirm the need for the reformation of the church in America. Gray said,

> "When the revival began, I thought it would be evangelistic, ministering to prostitutes, drug addicts, hurting people of the streets, but that did not happen... I realized God was doing a different thing here. Most everyone coming was just regular church people... people who were desperate, broken, hungry and hurting. They were born again, but their lives were a mess, and they needed to be rescued... we were not having a revival for lost souls. It was a revival for born-again people who needed to meet God again."

Gray sensed that God had now called him to be a "church health specialist," and bring backslidden believers back to their first love. Awakening is for the unbelievers, but revival is for stirring the hearts of a backslidden church.

The importance of holiness, consecration, and reckless devotion punctuated many of the sermons. This bold preacher in the cornfields proclaimed, "Empty yourself of everything that would grieve the Holy Spirit and return to your first love!"

Often, many were so overwhelmed by the preaching, they shook and fell to the floor. Some even collapsed while seated. No one touched them; they were just overpowered by the intensity of the sermon. Gray's messages cut deep and put many on their faces. People sensed that he meant business when he prayed, "Our lives for your life, Jesus!" It was time to give all to the Lord.

ONLY TIME FOR THE IMPORTANT THINGS

While outsiders were drawn to what was occurring at Smithton, insiders were even more compelled by the outworking of power. Many made personal sacrifices so that they could attend the weekly revival service. Hobbies, sports, television, and the movies did not interest them like they used to and fell by the wayside. No one asked people to give these things up; they just became more captivated by Jesus than anything else. One revival participant said, "We only made time for the important things—God, family, and work. Most everything else didn't matter."

Hundreds of people were reshuffling their priorities, and it was deepening the work of grace. Although Diane Daily worked her shift as nurse ten hours a day, she did not miss a single revival service. She arrived at church at 6pm on service nights and didn't make it home until 1:00 am. She woke up at 5:00 am and made her way to work, dreaming of getting back in the revival meeting that night.

Revivals are truly captivating. All your life is immersed in the things of the Kingdom. Only those who have encountered a true move of God understand this. When you're touched by the hand of God, He becomes your all. Nothing else; nothing less! A fierce devotion brings an intense fervor.

THUNDER IN OUR VOICES, LIGHTENING IN OUR EYES

Every evening, dozens of Smithton Community Church congregants rushed home from work and made their way to the services. Many arrived around 6pm to take part in pre-service prayer. Those gathered would intercede that God's presence would move through the room and the goodness and mercy of Jesus would transform hearts.

After finishing prayer, they would freshen up the room and get things ready for guests. Things needed to be wiped down, and the bathrooms cleaned. The sound system had to be turned on, properly mixed, and ready to blast the worship music.

Outside, hundreds of spiritually hungry people were waiting to get inside the building. Some had been standing in line since noon. These guests were eager to find their seats and be a part of what God was doing in the cornfields.

The night started with passionate worship. Eric and the musicians played with reckless abandon. Lyrics from one of the newly written songs proclaimed:

> "Thunder in their voices,
> lightening in their eyes,
> and when we speak the word, the dead will arise
> Spirit of revival! Spirit of revival!"

After worship, Gray would bring impassioned biblical messages. Hundreds would tremble as they heard these sermons. Groans would rise in the room as Gray shared what God was revealing to him through the text.

After the sermon, designated intercessors would emerge to minister to the people. They called these people "prayer warriors." The title was fitting, because within moments, the altar area looked like a war zone. As they prayed, the badged intercessors cried, "Now!" "God, display your power and might!" "More!" As they cried out, God's power was unleashed in the room.

In every service, demonized and tormented people were set free. Those receiving ministry were wide-eyed as they shook off chains—many falling with shrieks and convulsions. Most got up transformed. People left the service knowing they had been with Jesus and they were coming alive again.

People in the services were being touched in countless ways. Some would scream or speak in tongues. Other fell out as the glory of the Lord overpowered them. Intense weeping was common. Sometimes violent shaking begun and continued for days. Others were "frozen in place" in a trance-like state. Dozens had to be carried out in many of the services. One observer remarked:

> "People would respond en masse even during the worship time running to the front of the building, filling the front from the platform to the first row and up the aisles about three quarters of the way to the back of the auditorium. The presence of God was so mighty… people fell on all sides… Pastor Steve stepped down and touched a couple of men. Then he got jolted from the platform all the way into the front row… people from nine to sixty years old—teens and middle aged—all went down by the power of God."

Other pilgrims who had come to Missouri to encounter the revival shared similar reports. One wrote,

> "We saw demonized, tormented people set free… there was… strong shaking and falling down with… shrieks and… convulsions… when the people got up off the floor, they were happy, bright and fully recovered."

The services would often last until midnight or one in the morning. Even as Gray and his team tried to shut things down, most didn't want to leave. More than once, a visitor pleaded to stay in the building all night.

THE CROWDS

After *Charisma Magazine* published a news story about the revival in early 1997, people from across the Midwest made their way to this backwater town. Seekers traveled from St. Louis, Columbia, and Kansas City. Soon van loads were also driving in from Omaha, Minneapolis, and Chicago. On weekends, the out-of-town folks often outnumbered the locals by three to one.

As hundreds of visitors arrived, the old meetinghouse was stretched to its limit. They packed people in shoulder-to-shoulder, and ushers pulled out folding chairs. By the revival's eleventh week, services were moved to the gymnasium. The old sanctuary continued to be used as an overflow room. Amazing scenes continued to echo through the walls.

Sometimes the line of cars arriving at the church stretched from the intersection of Clay and Chestnut streets for two-and-a-half miles to Highway 50. Gray told the congregation, in the early years, "Imagine people lining up to get in," and his far-fetched prediction became a reality.

They squeezed together automobiles and lined them up and down the streets. If a carload arrived early, they couldn't leave at the end of the service. Their car would be locked in behind other vehicles. This is part of the reason the church had to have ushers.

Every weekend, there were more people and cars than the grounds could accommodate. Although the worshippers were squeezed together and could barely move, they hardly noticed the inconveniences. Underneath it all, they were thrilled to be a part of a powerful move of God.

Over the next few years, visitors from fifty states and seventy nations visited Smithton. In the jam-packed room, one found farmers, factory workers, and mechanics. Beside them, one would also find denominational officials, businessmen, and doctors. Men with doctorates in theology received prayer from 16-year-olds. Young and old and people with different ethnicities wept together. God was doing an unexpected work in the cornfields of West-Central Missouri.

MEDIA TALKS ABOUT THE REVIVAL

Testimonies were shared and various members of the news media descended on the outpouring. *Charisma Magazine* was already mentioned, but reporters from *Christianity Today, 700 Club, It's Supernatural,* and other international and denominational publications descended on tiny little Smithton.

Later, *Time Magazine, Newsweek, St. Louis Post-Dispatch,* and the *Kansas City Star* dispatched journalists to the revival. Multitudes were intrigued by what God was doing in small town America.

Several journalists were impacted by the move of God. When a reporter from Christian Broadcasting Network came to report on the revival, he barely witnessed what occurred. By the second worship song, the power of God hit him so hard that he collapsed to the floor. He laid there, "out in the spirit," for the rest of the evening. He was delighted with what he encountered.

Not all the media figures understood what was occurring, but they sensed that this was something extraordinary. This felt like a throwback to the old frontier revivals and the amazing stories hidden in dusty old history books.

IMPACTING CHURCHES

As the revival burned hot in Smithton, hundreds of ministry leaders came to see what the fuss was all about. Some of them were hungry for a fresh move of God, but others came to mock and criticize what was occurring. Sometimes a minister would come in as a skeptic and change their mind when they witnessed the amazing things.

Many were inexplicably transformed in the Missouri cornfields. One small town Alabama pastor had lost most of his people in his congregation. All he had left was one couple. In desperation, he traveled to Smithton and was overcome by the majesty of Jesus. When he returned home, he brought the fires of revival. It wasn't long before God had breathed new life into his church. One year later, the sanctuary was full, and hundreds were in pursuit of God.

Hundreds of out-of-state pastors experienced fresh fire and brought it home to their congregations. Sometimes a leader would not feel like anything changed after he spent a weekend in Smithton, but as soon as he returned home, and stood in the pulpit, something erupted. One said, "Something had obviously come over me and the people could sense it as soon as I opened my mouth."

With so much going on in Smithton, word also began to spread overseas. Believers from Japan, Israel, Philippines, Korea, Singapore, Germany, Canada, and England began traveling across oceans to visit this tiny little town. The rustling cornfields became international.

On one weekend, Korean guests wanted to see the exact spot where Gray was struck by God's power. When they were shown the place, in the old meetinghouse, they placed their faces on the carpet and pleaded with the Lord to come to their nation. There wasn't a dry eye in the room after witnessing such stupendous hunger.

Witnessing people from Europe, Asia, and Latin America was overwhelming to the congregation. Although they prayed people would come from the north, south, east, and west, this was more spectacular than they imagined.

SIGNS AND WONDERS

In this glorious revival, there were hundreds of miraculous encounters, but most of these marvelous stories were never recorded. A genuine move of God doesn't fixate on the sensational. People should, instead, focus on Jesus, not bizarre experiences. Nevertheless, there were unusual things unfolding as the people gathered in this country town.

Sometimes people would witness what they described as a "glory cloud." It looked like a "light-filled fog" floated near the ceiling. When it rolled in, there was a "weightiness." Everyone had to bow down or fall to the floor. Witnessing this, one man from Kansas thought the church was pumping strange gas into the room through the air conditioning ducts. He raced out the door and locked himself in his car. He never considered that a poor country church couldn't afford something that elaborate.

Also, the children told their parents they saw angels in the services. One said that she saw two nine-foot angels move through the room at the end of the sermon as Pastor Steve Gray called people to commit to the Lord. It would seem that these heavenly beings were a part of the heavenly entourage, drawing the people closer to Jesus. The Bible calls God the "Lord of Hosts." Wherever he goes, His attendants come with Him.

An Assemblies of God pastor from Michigan claimed he had an open vision during the worship one Friday night. He watched as what appeared to be a ladder came down through the back wall and hundreds of angels rushed into the room. Each wanted to be the first to worship with the people. He said that they looked elated to glorify God with all the revival participants.

An unbeliever once came to the revival intent on causing a disturbance. Shortly after the worship began, he was agitated and shaken. Jumping out of his seat, he made a hasty retreat, running as fast as he could toward the back door. Once outside, he shouted to those still arriving, "You shouldn't enter this place because there are angels running up and down the aisle!" He then continued running down the street until he disappeared out of sight.

One hot July night, Gray began ministering to those who had gathered for the revival. He focused on their physical needs. While all of this was going on, the drummer of the church was sitting in the overflow room. His back had been thrown out, and the doctor told him he couldn't pick up his seven-year-old daughter or hold a gallon of milk. The drummer had a huge velcro back brace and a walker.

This injured musician had been watching the healing ministry transpire on the screen, and he wanted to receive prayer. However, because he was slow, he couldn't make it into the room until the healing ministry was almost over. He pushed open the door with his walker, and five hundred people turned to see him hobble in. The entire room erupted in intercession. The drummer moved slowly, and the rattle of the rickety walker could be heard with every step. As he approached, Gray embraced him and the two fell to the ground in an act of spontaneous intercession. The drummer's wife's eyes got as big as saucers because she knew that it was dangerous for him fall to the ground like that. However, about ten seconds later, the injured drummer leaped up, pulled off his Velcro back brace, and picked up his young daughter. He danced across the front of the sanctuary, completely healed.

Hundreds of marvelous breakthroughs occurred in the revival services. People were forever changed in the presence of the Lord.

THE REVIVAL SPREADS

News of what God was doing in Smithton spread and arrested the attention of global ministry leaders. Many wanted to hear about the church's glorious encounters in the presence of God.

Warren Marcus, who worked with Christian Broadcasting Network and 700 Club, visited the revival and filmed a documentary called "Go Inside the Smithton Outpouring." He recruited Sid Roth to be the moderator and filmed the revival services in Smithton. This film captivated the hearts of all who watched it, and was even viewed internationally.

Denominations and ministry groups wanted the Grays to speak. At first, the Grays were invited to share at major conferences in the U.S. Then foreign leaders began to reach out to them. This dynamic couple was invited to minister in Japan, Australia, New Zealand, England, and other parts of the world. The anointing of the Smithton Outpouring was being carried to the nations.

Signs and miracles were also transpiring in their travels. After preaching a message in Japan, Gray was in a back room when a group of men barged in. A demonized woman was in the sanctuary screaming, writhing, and biting. They wanted his help, expecting to see a wild demonstration, but Gray calmly approached her. He held out his hand and said, "Shalom." At that moment, the woman was filled with peace and love, and the name of Jesus was magnified.

Many other remarkable things took place as the Grays told the remarkable story of what God had done in their rural congregation. Entire rooms of people would be struck down as Gray shared his biblical insights.

Spreading the message of revival to other lands was thrilling, but the move of God at Smithton remained Gray's top priority. He could have gained more notoriety, but he refused to walk away from his beloved congregation. The people meant everything to him.

DON'T DESPISE SMALL BEGINNINGS

In many ways, the Smithton Outpouring was reminiscent of the powerful revivals that occurred generations ago. A distinguishing reader will find many commonalities with the Cane Ridge Camp meeting, the Welsh revival, and the early Pentecostal meetings. Not everyone understood the magnitude of what God was doing in the cornfields, but a few did.

This work of God was unmistakable. Over three-and-a-half years, a quarter of a million people poured into a small Missouri town from around the world. The Smithton Outpouring torched the earth as multitudes carried the fire from that small place back to their congregations.

A quarter of a century later, you will still hear a pastor talk about the "desperation" that he witnessed in the revival services at Smithton.

God does marvelous things. He stirred multitudes from the tiny town of Smithton, and he is still doing wonders on the earth. Never despise the day of small beginnings.

> "For the vision is yet for an appointed time; but at the end it will speak, and it will not lie. Though it tarries, wait for it; because it will surely come, it will not tarry." (Habakkuk 2:3)

KANSAS CITY REVIVAL

Steve Gray ministering in Kansas City

"What is needed in this hour is a great outpouring of the Holy Spirit and mouthpieces willing to reveal the mysteries of the Kingdom." —J. D. King

"Revival is people being immersed, inundated, overflowing, saturated, controlled by, carried by, and lead by the Holy Spirit."
—Kathy Gray

"Brethren it is just so much humbug to be waiting for this, night after night, month after month, if we ourselves are not right with God. I must ask myself—'Is my heart pure? Are my hands clean?'"—Donald John Smith in the Hebrides Revival

"The price is high. God does not want partnership with us but ownership of us." —Leonard Ravenhill

"Professing Christians must be brought to realize that the preeminent desire and demand of God for us is that of the continual pursuit of the holiness of life, and the reflection of His holiness. 'Be ye holy, for I am holy.'"—Herbert Lockyer, Sr.

"Conspicuous holiness ought to be the mark of the Church of God. A holy church has God in the midst of her."—Charles H. Spurgeon

A visiting pastor from Iowa approached Pastor Steve Gray in late 1999 and asked, "When has God ever moved a revival? Who do you think you are, moving your ministry somewhere else?" The Smithton Outpouring had been going strong for three-and-a-half years, and thousands had received fresh touches from the Lord. Many wanted to venture to the Missouri wilderness to see what was blowing in the wind.

When Gray first contemplated relocating, the idea seemed absurd. *Hosanna Integrity* had just released a live worship album from the revival and Gray wrote the best-selling *When the Kingdom*

Comes: Lessons from the Smithton Outpouring. Why would anyone want to mess up the accolades they were receiving?

But Gray doesn't think like other men. He was willing to do anything that God led him to do. He had uprooted his life a few times before and knew that unwavering obedience was vital.

As Gray contemplated his exit, people were criticizing him. One reporter asked him if he thought the revival would end if he left. He said that it would most certainly end if they didn't advance with God. Like ancient Israel, Gray and his team needed to follow the fire to the promised land.

Is a revival tied to the land or is it rooted in the hearts of the people? Gray believed that those who had been impacted in the revival carried the fervor. It was not locked into a particular zip code or building.

FOLLOW THE FIRE

In the fourth year of the Smithton Outpouring, changes were unfolding. Many could feel it in the air. Gray sensed that God was speaking to him, but he didn't understand all that was going on.

Some badly needed insight came after Steve and Kathy returned from a ministry trip to Asia. As they drove over the railroad tracks on the edge of town, both felt a "shift in the Spirit." God moved unusually, revealing new avenues He wanted them to pursue.

A lot of different things were coming together at that moment. Gray was being sought as a conference speaker on the national level. He understood the realities of the Kingdom that transformed churches. The Grays were moving up, but the town of Smithton was becoming antagonistic.

From the beginning, there was discontent about the throngs of strangers pouring into the town. Locals didn't like all the noise and the traffic.

One time Kathy had to run from her car to the church because she was bombarded by beer cans thrown by local naysayers. Sometimes people from across the street yelled and cursed. That was part of revival life. The townspeople wanted their quiet community back. One disgruntled resident said, "I live two blocks away and can't sit on my front porch without having to hear that raucous music every night."

The discontent wasn't just in the neighbors. Something dark raised its ugly head from within. A few families wanted to go back to the way things were before the revival. They liked it when everything was slower and the church wasn't open all the time. Opposition was increasing within and without. People think that revival causes division, but it merely shines a light on the divisions that are already there.

Many didn't understand the intensity and fervor. They couldn't understand why anyone would truly make Jesus the center of everything. Christians claim to value God, but their value systems show that He is not the most important part of their lives. The Grays and the Smithton faithful were truly focused on the Kingdom of God.

Along the streets of Smithton, bitterness arose. It was like a cancer that spread through the bloodstream. People criticized and complained to their neighbors. Even a few of the members turned against the move of God.

Thousands of spiritually hungry people were coming to Smithton from around the globe, but many within the community cursed the ground that the church was built on.

The Grays sensed that the revival would wane if they stayed in Smithton, and they didn't want the fire to die. At that time, the Lord spoke to Kathy and told her, in the words of the Prophet Jeremiah, to "Flee Babylon."

"Flee from Babylon!
    Run for your lives!

Do not be destroyed because of her sins.
It is time for the Lord's vengeance;
he will repay her what she deserves"
(Jeremiah 51:6 NIV).

This disruptive nudge from the Lord was bewildering to Steve and Kathy. Were they supposed to uproot things? Was God calling them to transition the outpouring to a different location? When has anyone in history moved a revival? This was unprecedented.

As Steve sought the Lord, he got a picture of ancient Israel journeying through the wilderness to a new place. The only sense of direction that they had was a cloud by day and a pillar of fire by night. They didn't have all the answers, but they were willing to follow the Lord.

One night, in deep prayer, Gray asked God if he would give him a guarantee of continued revival if he moved. He wrote,

> "I asked the Lord, if we moved, would He guarantee that revival would continue? His only pledge was that if we didn't obey, the revival in Smithton would end. We were not moving to be successful; we were moving to be obedient."

Gray knew that they were going to have to follow the fire. God was transitioning the ministry to a new territory. But where would they go?

GOIN' TO KANSAS CITY

Columbia, the home of the University of Missouri was less than an hour away. Some thought the church should go there. Others mentioned Springfield—thousands of Pentecostals lived in that community and they were praying for a fresh move of God. But these places were not where the leaders felt drawn. Kansas City, almost one hundred miles away, was the destination that the Lord laid on their hearts.

Gray began to share his new vision with the congregation. He explained to them the mighty move of God wasn't ending; it was being repositioned to burn even hotter. He knew that the way they responded in this moment was going to shape their destiny. He told them that the Lord had put Kansas City on their hearts and they were going to follow the fire.

Moving from summer into the fall, they held the last outpouring services in Smithton. Hundreds of people jammed into the building to be a part of the final gatherings in this tiny town. As the glory of the Lord burst through the building, many still wondered whether it was wise to leave. The services were still so explosive. Why risk something so precious?

SETBACKS AND STRUGGLES

Relocating seventy different families and a thriving local ministry isn't easy. The people who wanted to relocate needed to sell homes, resign jobs, and find new employment in Kansas City. There were a lot of moving pieces. Wrong choices could easily shut down the momentum.

Making things more difficult was the fact that they were moving from a rural farm community to a large city. In a metropolitan area, houses were nearly double the price, and land was difficult to come by.

After spying out the land, Gray negotiated with a large Baptist church to lease their old sanctuary. It was in a centrally located suburb and could seat 1,200 people. The building had plenty of office space and classrooms. This seemed to be exactly what the congregation needed.

Everything appeared to be in order, but the Baptist church's governing board rejected the deal because they didn't like what was taking place in the revival meetings. The elders were afraid that their church would be associated with "tongue-talkers and crazy Charismatics."

Gray was ready to get things up and running when he got the news that they would not let them lease the building. It felt like a kick in the stomach. Families had already moved, and they had no place to hold services. This obstacle was unsettling. If things got delayed, would the fire of revival still be burning? Was this all a mistake?

Gray knew he heard the voice of God and that he had to keep his eyes on what was before him. As tempting as it was to move everything back to Smithton, he kept moving forward. Kansas City was going to be their new home, one way or another.

Excitement rose when they found another building off I-470 in Grandview, Missouri. This massive edifice had been a lumber yard and home remodeling warehouse. There was plenty of room to grow and lots of opportunity with this building. People were excited about this development.

Once again, Gray's plans were dashed. The day before the papers would be signed, corporate lawyers discovered they did not have the right to sub-lease to a not-for-profit corporation. This strategically placed building slipped out of their hands, too. This was so disheartening. Would the congregation ever be able to set up shop in Kansas City? Would the revival's fervor be lost?

That night Gray stormed heaven in prayer. He reminded God that he had followed his leading and now he felt like everything was collapsing around him. Families already moved to Kansas City and people were questioning the wisdom of his decision. This pastor pled with God for wisdom and direction.

Amid prayers of desperation, Gray heard the Lord speak: "Cover the city in glory!" He then knew what he was supposed to do—begin holding services in other churches in Kansas City. The Lord showed him that he was to host weekend outpouring services in places across the metro area—covering the city in glory. Gray explained, "What if we went to local churches, taking our entire congregation, sound system, worship team and all, and held revival services in their facilities."

Several churches were open to the idea. The displaced Smithton flock would now gather in Gardiner, Kansas, Lee's Summit, Missouri, Blue Springs, Missouri, and Kansas City, Missouri.

The seed for the burgeoning Kansas City revival was planted. Through the unwavering faith of Gray, the seemingly impossible plan unfolded and the rumblings of revival could once again be heard in the heartland.

PAULA HUTCHESON

God is often at work long before we see his hand. On April 7, 1985—Easter Sunday—a young woman wanted to take advantage of a beautiful Hawaiian day. As she was sunbathing at the beach, she heard the sounds of a man nearby. A preacher was addressing a group of people who had come to the ocean for a Sunday service and baptisms.

As she listened to his proclamation of the gospel, her heart stirred. Watching men and women come out of the water, changed, affected her. She wanted to encounter the gospel, too. Gasping for breath and tears streaming down her eyes, she ran over to be baptized. She was brought into the Kingdom in a bikini and a "mai-tai" in her hand.

This newly redeemed woman's name was Paula, and she did not yet know what God had called her to accomplish in the years ahead.

God blessed Paula and brought her into the realm of real estate. Millions of dollars worth of property were placed into her hands. People would sign rental units over to her and give her access to unimaginable deals.

After she moved to Kansas City, she started a company named "God's Property," and acquired multiple properties in the metro. Paula's Jewish attorney told her that he never heard of people giving away properties. Other realtors complimented Paula on her business acumen, but she told them that it had nothing to do with her.

Although Paula wasn't certain about everything, she knew God was doing something. Behind the scenes, the Lord was preparing the way for an influx of people from Smithton, Missouri who needed a home.

In the fall of 1999, a colleague asked Paula if she wanted to visit the revival services in Smithton. She was told about the lives being changed and the tangible presence of God that was felt in the place. Paula didn't know what her colleague was talking about, but if God was there, it was worth checking out.

The revival was beginning its transition toward Kansas City and Paula could not make it to the services. However, some of the families relocating from Smithton got in touch with her.

Mary McClain, an intercessor and active member of Smithton Community Church was one of the first to reach out to Paula. She noticed an ad in the *Raytown Post* and called. Mary told Paula the group that she was associated with, and the realtor was flabbergasted. There was no way in the natural this could transpire. Paula began wondering what God was doing.

The next morning, when Paula arrived at her office, she found five individuals sitting on her steps. Mary McClain had told them about her and they traveled over one hundred miles to speak with her.

The pastoral team from the Smithton congregation soon sent dozens of people needing homes her way. Most had no jobs and very little money, but Paula was able to assist them. She waived security deposits and delayed rent payments—going out of her way to assist a displaced congregation.

God helped the Smithton families, providing homes and provision. And Paula, who was just trying to be faithful to the Lord, was blessed as well. She became an active member of the church as it gained its footing in the Kansas City metro. God was clearly at work in all of this.

COVER THE CITY IN GLORY

Pastor Steve Gray pressed forward, even when it seemed like things were unraveling. After several buildings fell through, they met in the sanctuaries of other congregations. God had told him to, "Cover the city in glory." This became something of a revival tour, and many visitors from around the United States attended these services.

The first church was in Gardner, Kansas, in the southwest corner of the Kansas City metro. Gray wondered if anyone would come, and was surprised to see a multitude of guests. Visitors from the metro and fourteen other states were lined up around the building when he arrived on the property. Kathy Gray began the meeting with a remembrance of the things God had done and wanted to do again:

> "Look what He did for us, out in the middle of nowhere. Over the past four years... we have been visited by over seventy nations. Thousands and thousands of people have found their way to a church in the middle of nowhere. We have seen the glory of God. We have seen them lined up around the building, waiting to get inside... I have seen times when the people... would collapse like wheat blown by a hard wind... collapsing under the glory of God. I have seen the hand of God work so many miracles and healings... He wants to renew His deeds in our day more than we want it."

It was a weekend of glory and grace. There were many healings and deliverances. The congregation was reignited and new life began flowing in the room. The glory cloud had moved from Smithton and revival fire once again was in full swing.

Next stop was the Harmony Vineyard in North Kansas City. Wonderful manifestations of God's power also exploded in this church. People were falling and shaking as the powerful works of the Lord erupted through the crowds. The inidivduals from the Vineyard church and other congregations were lined up to receive a fresh touch of God.

Over the next few months, the Smithton congregants continued gathering, from church to church. It was thrilling to see what God was doing in all the different places, but it was quite laborious to set up and break down every weekend. All of the uncertainty was exhausting on the Smithton faithful. The congregation needed their own building.

The last weeks of the "Cover the City in Glory" tour were held at Christ Triumphant Church in Lee's Summit, Missouri. This congregation was also hungry for revival and their pastor was gracious. He went out of his way to accommodate Gray and the Smithton refugees.

Christ Triumphant Church had also had a stirring from the Lord on March 24, 1996—the same day as the revival erupted in Smithton. On that Sunday, God visited this Lee's Summit congregation and turned things upside down. The glory fell in the building and many were laid out under the power. The pastor was ready to move forward in revival, but many of the people resisted it. He was saddened at the lost opportunity.

So when the members of the Smithton congregation wanted to meet at his church, he jumped at the opportunity. He would not stop until revival erupted in Christ Triumphant Church.

A PLACE TO LAND

After months of searching, Gray and his leadership team found sixty-two acres of wooded land in the southeast corner of Kansas City, facing I-470. This would be a perfect place to construct a building and expand the ministry. But would they be able to purchase this land? Although they saved money, it wasn't all that sizable. Gray met with the landowner and recounted the story of the revival. He explained his vision for the land and told the old man how much money they had to spend. Surprisingly, the landowner agreed to the amount. God did a miraculous work.

At long last, the revivalists had found the promised land, but they didn't have a building, or additional money. They scrounged together enough to purchase a large "circus" tent. The tattered, mildewed ediface wasn't much on the eyes. In fact, Steve and Kathy gasped when they first saw it. They said, "People thought we were a 'circus show' before. I wonder what they are going to say now?"

On the fourth of July weekend in 2000, the revival services began again on the newly acquired property. One thousand people crowded into the tent, amid scorching heat, to help launch what would become World Revival Church.

The presence of God overwhelmed the people as they gathered under the canvas flaps. Some claimed that the glory was even greater than what they had encountered in Smithton. Many witnessed what they described as "the glory cloud" floating at the top of the tent. There weren't many dry eyes in the room as the people fervently interceded and worshipped.

Some of the men from the church covered the floor of the tent with sand and green astroturf. Everything was fairly primitive. To minimize the intensity of the heat, the ministry purchased six multi-ton air conditioners to pump cool air into the tent. But it was hard to keep things comfortable when temperatures were over one hundred degrees. It was scorching but the people didn't care. They just wanted to encounter God.

ENCOUNTERS CONTINUE

People from across America, and even as far away as Egypt, attended the services. License plates from several states graced the gravel parking lot. The hunger witnessed in Smithton continued in Kansas City. God did not withhold his hand.

As the weekend unfolded, explosive worship music poured out from thin fabric walls—overflowing into the parking lot and mingling with the roar of air conditioners. The sounds gave one the sense of being at an outdoor concert. A group of men from out of state were filled with anticipation. One said,

> "As we entered the side rear door of the tent we immediately were bent over, doubled at the waist. What was this? We had never felt anything like this before. It was as if a hundred pound weight was dropped on our shoulders. All three of us were bent over and could hardly walk until we became accustomed to the atmosphere. The Jews called it the 'KABAD, 'the weightiness of God, and it surrounded and covered us like a thick woolen blanket and we began to understand the deeper things of God. These humble people, here in Kansas City, had opened a portal between heaven and earth and were experiencing a habitation of the glory of God."

The presence of the Holy Spirit touched hundreds. If one came into the tent, they could not escape the convicting power of the Lord. A group of Methodists came one night and made the following testimony:

> "We have found new life and we will take this back to our home churches. We truly have a hunger for God. John Wesley had it, and we want it again! Jesus said, 'it is time!'"

At one meeting, Gray asked for everyone who wanted to be baptized in the Holy Spirit to come forward. The front was so crowded rows of chairs had to be removed. Gray told them that when he said, "Receive the Spirit" they were to speak in tongues. After praying a prayer of acceptance and sanctification, he shouted, "Receive the Spirit now!" Instantly, every person in the tent started praising the Lord in heavenly languages.

Often, in the altar time at the end of the service, the heavens opened and the noise of prayer warriors mingled with agonizing cries. These noises, and the wind of the Spirit, made a sound so holy it could never be forgotten.

As a mother and daughter ran forward for prayer, the daughter "suddenly flew backward two or three feet—as though she ran into a wall." The mother stopped and put out her index finger, encountering a "soft barrier." When she pressed harder, it was like pushing against a balloon.

What was astounding in these meetings was that the prayer warriors seldom laid hands on people. What the crowds were encountering, during this time of ministry, was a collision of the Spirit. It was the in-breaking of the kingdom of God.

People felt the tangible presence of God. One visitor was so frightened by it that he ran out of the tent. When he finally came back in, he made his way to the front and fell to the floor. One visitor wrote:

> "I had already been prayed for. Lifting myself off the floor, I noticed one of the leaders praying. He was surrounded, like a fort, by a circle of bodies on top of each other, two to three high. I decided I wanted to get some of what he was imparting. Making my way, I was about ten feet from him when he looked at me. Throwing his hand out toward me, he said, 'Take it.' Whatever it was, it was like I was hit by something big. I flew back three feet—into the front row of chairs. God did a wonderful work in me."

As the services continued, the Holy Spirit moved in staggering ways with healings, deliverances, restored marriages, and people rediscovering hope. One participant shared the following testimony:

"The worship was overwhelming. The presence of God came in like a flood and you had to hold on to the metal chair in front of you to keep from being pushed backwards by a spiritual flow. It was like the ebbing and rushing waves of the tide. Then a strong wind of the Spirit would blow and you could see the people weave back and forth in unison like a Kansas wheat field blown in the wind. It was over 100 degrees outside but cool and refreshing inside the tent, but when you raised your hands a few feet above your head, you could feel the heat. We would jokingly say, 'Hey, raise your hands and feel the fire of God.'"

Whether the weather was good or bad, it made little difference. Tornados and thunder storms passed through, but people kept coming. A few times, strong winds knocked over some of the equipment and the tent had to be shored up, but God covered them and kept them from serious damage.

Several nights a week, the tent was packed, and the floor was covered with the sobbing masses. During praise and worship, the presence of the Lord increased. Instead of heartless singing, the people heard a "holy roar." Some said it sounded like "mighty rushing waters." Across the tent, people fell, and entire rows were on their knees. Most were laid out, but some held on to poles or anything stationary to keep from collapsing. The hearts were so full that they felt like bursting.

BUILDING A BUILDING

Gray was determined to get a building up before the cold winter season. When he said he was going to get the sanctuary built in six months, people laughed. Architects and city officials said, "It will take a least two years to get through all the city codes." Gray said, "I don't have that long. We need a building right away!"

Miracle after miracle occurred to make way for this project. At first, the Kansas City administrators would not sign off on the plans, but after intense prayer, they changed their minds. Though low on money, the ministry was able purchase the metal trusses and fixtures for reasonable prices.

Along with the experienced builders, teams from the congregation worked hard to erect the sanctuary. Some took it upon themselves to work late into the night and helped on weekends.

Few thought that Gray and his congregation could get a sanctuary up so quickly, but they were convinced God would back them up. Their hopes were finally realized. The congregation gained occupancy on the building on January 5, 2001, just as temperatures dropped below zero.

To the congregation, it was like entering the Holy of Holies as they walked through the doors of their new sanctuary. The people were so enthralled by the goodness and favor of God.

The services continued to be punctuated by the movement of the Holy Spirit. Deliverances, healings, and salvations were transpiring every weekend. Notable men came to participate in this stupendous outpouring: including Pat Roberson, Steve Hill, John Kilpatrick, Lindell Cooley, Rodney Howard-Browne, Claudio Freidzon, Carlos Annacondia, Mike Bickle, Sid Roth, and Jim Goll.

Crowds from across the globe continued to come to Kansas City to encounter the flames of revival. The Grays nurtured and guided the revival, trusting in scripture and the leadings of the Lord. They poured out their lives serving the people and keeping the flame burning. Gray once said,

> "We've spent times ourselves repenting and turning to the Lord and adjusting our priorities and examining our hearts. It's been like our own housecleaning. I didn't want to host the revival and have my own congregation unstable or anything like that."

Gray and his team maintained the revival atmosphere for

several years and made the deeper encounters sustainable. People came back year after year, astounded that the presence and glory of the Lord remained. One visiting pastor said, "Somehow they have found a way to move from a visitation to a habitation."

THE RESURGENCE

After some measure of waning after the building was opened, the Spirit of God broke open in 2008. Suddenly, World Revival Church experienced a wondrous revival resurgence. The outpouring of the Holy Spirit had broken open once again.

On May 2, 2008, Gray addressed the congregation, reminding them of the importance of heartfelt worship. He called everyone to go to a deeper place. While he was speaking, the fresh wind of the Spirit blew through the room and hundreds were overcome. Some shook and wept with heavy tears. Others were gripped with a spirit of travail. A few felt the surge of fresh empowerment. They stood up and prophesied the heart of the Lord.

In one service, a nine-year-old boy began praying and exhorting so dynamically that seasoned prayer warriors collapsed. People whose hearts had grown cold came back to the Lord, giving their lives fully to the message of the Kingdom. The sounds of revival could be heard once more as the people repented and groaned before God.

During the altar ministry at the end of the service, masses of people would sprint to the front. Some would leap over chairs and move past people—wanting to be the first to receive prayer. Several times spiritually hungry people jumped over disabled people in wheelchairs, hungry for a fresh touch from God. Dozens tore the skin off their nose as they slid across the floor. They were so desperate for God that they didn't care that their blood was dripping on the floor. Gray made the following observation:

> "God's conviction, along with the intense desire among people wanting to be near Jesus, causes crowds to rush the altar. I'm not standing there telling them to repent. The conviction just comes in and people want to change. There's repentance, there's brokenness, there's sincerity, there's power, and then the Lord just sweeps through."

Marcus Lamb, the president of the Daystar Christian Television Network, attended the revival meetings in Kansas City one night and said, "This is a true revival. This is a revival of integrity and righteousness. Some of you need to think about paying the way to send your pastors to World Revival Church."

Lamb and his Daystar team were so enamored with what was occurring that they arranged to broadcast the Friday evening services from Kansas City live. They brought out a satellite truck and aired the wonderful things that God was doing. Tens of thousands from around the world watched the services and were overwhelmed with the majesty of the Lord. More than once, so many calls came into the Daystar call center that the system crashed and remained off line for hours.

God has continued to use this congregation to touch the hearts and minds of men. The culture of revival that has been cultivated through these families continued to affect countless numbers of people in Kansas City and in other parts of the world.

Steve and Kathy Gray and those who have stood alongside them have been believing for a greater release of the Kingdom of God in our generation. They not only want to see revival, but also a reformation that transforms the attitude of believers around the world. It is time for everyone who claims the name of

Jesus to turn their hearts and minds back to the Lord. Gray once declared,

> "Right now many churches are fighting a battle they cannot win because they are fighting in the flesh. But God is raising up a chosen Church birthed in the Holy Spirit, and she will win the war. We will go from being victims to victors, from weak to strong, from divided to united, from lazy to loyal... this is the day of the coming Kingdom, and we must listen for the windows of heaven as they open. God is extending the greatest opportunity any of us has ever received, and I trust that as He continues to speak to your heart, you will traverse beyond what you have known in your Christian life and begin to walk in the power and presence of our King."

Revival is much more than shouting and enjoying exciting church services. It's not merely raised hands and passionate singing. A real outpouring of the Holy Spirit facilitates a deep encounter with the Lord that transforms everything in the lives of people.

Steve and Kathy Gray walked through the dark night of the soul and came out on the other side. They emerged from the wilderness, encountering the overwhelming beauty and grace of the Lord. They have taught us, in revival, the distracted and disobedient look upon the face of Jesus, and are changed.

> "For now we see only a reflection as in a mirror; then we shall see face to face. Now I know in part; then I shall know fully, even as I am fully known" (1 Corinthians 13:12).

EPILOGUE

"We have heard it with our ears, O God; our ancestors have told us what you did in their days, in days long ago" (Psalm 44:1 NIV).

～

T he marvelous stories have not ended. God is ready to rend the heavens and come down once again. I believe that the world is on the verge of the greatest spiritual awakening it has ever experienced. The shaking is about to begin.

Can you feel it? Can you hear it? Listen . . . Do you hear the thunder in the distance? That is the rumblings of revival.

—Frank "J. J." DiPietro

BIBLIOGRAPHY

Several books, articles, online research sites, and personal interviews were utilized in the development of *Rend the Heavens*. Here is a select list of these works.

Bounds, E.M. *Prayer.* New Kensington, PA: Whitaker House, 1997.

Brim, Billye. *First of All And The Awakenings.* Branson, MO: Billie Brim Ministries, 2017.

Campbell, Duncan. *Revival in the Hebrides.* CreateSpace, 2016.

Conkin, Paul K. *Cane Ridge: America's Pentecost. Madison, Wisconsin:* University of Wisconsin Press, 1990.

Dallimore, Arnold. *George Whitefield (2 Vol).* Edinburg, Scotland: Banner of Truth Trust, 1970.

Di Pietro, Frank. *The Fire That Once Was.* Lee's Summit, MO: Christos Publishing, 2020.

Duewel, Wesley. *Revival Fire.* Grand Rapids, MI: Zondervan, 1995.

Edwards, Jonathan. *Life and Diary of David Brainerd*. Peabody, MA: Hendrickson Publishing, 2006.

Gray, Steve. *When the Kingdom Comes*, Grand Rapids, MI: Chosen Books, 1999.

Gray, Steve. Follow the Fire. Lake Mary, FL: Charisma House, 2001.

Holmes, Frank. *Brother Indeed: The Life of Robert Cleaver Chapman*. Kilmarnoch, Scotland: John Ritchie LTD., 1988.

Jenson, Florence Huntington. *Hearts Aflame*, Waukesha, WISC: Metropolitan Church Association, 1932.

Kilpatrick, John. *Feast of Fire*, Pensacola, FL: Brownsville Assembly of God, 1995.

Kilpatrick, John. *When the Heavens are Brass*, Harrisburg, PA.: Destiny Image Publishers, 1997.

Lairdon, Roberts. *God's Generals: The Missionaries*. New Kensington, PA: Whitaker House, 2014.

McGatlin, Ron. *I saw the Smithton Outpouring*. Mt. Airy, N.C.: Basileia Publishers, 2002.

McNemar, Richard. *The Kentucky Revival*. Trumpet Press, 2012.

Orr, Edwin J. *The Event of the Century: The 1857-1858 Awakening*, Wheaton, IL: International Awakening Press, 1989.

Paisley, Ian R.K. *The 'Fifty Nine" Revival*. Belfast, Ireland: Martyrs Memorial Free Presbyterian Church, 1987.

Peckham, Colin and Mary. *Sounds From Heaven: The Revival on the Isle of Lewis 1949-1952*. Ross-Shire, Scotland: Christian Focus Publications, 2004.

Pratney, Winkie. *Revival*. Lindale, Texas: Agape Force, 1984.

Ravenhill, Leonard. *Why Revival Tarries*. Minneapolis, Minnesota: Bethany House, 1987.

Ravenhill, Leonard. *Revival Praying*. Grand Rapids, Michigan: Baker Publishing Group, 2005.

Ravenhill, Leonard. *Revival God's Way*, Minneapolis, Minnesota: Bethany House Publishers, 1983.

Sidwell, Mark. *Faith of Our Fathers: Scenes From Church History*. Greenville, SC: Bob Jones University Press, 1989.

Spurgeon, Charles H. *The Treasury of David*. Grand Rapids, MI: Kregel Publications, 1976.

Steer, Robert. *Hudson Taylor: A Man in Christ*. London: Hodder & Strouhton, 1990.

Taylor, Howard. *Hudson Taylor's Spiritual Secret*. Chicago, Il: Moody Bible Institute, 1989.

Walters, Kathie. *Bright and Shining Revival*. Macon, GA.: Good News Fellowship Ministries, 2000.

Whitaker, Colin. *Great Revivals*. London: Marshall Pickering, 1990.

ABOUT THE AUTHOR

Frank "J. J." Di Pietro, before becoming an independent researcher and author, spent several decades in radio broadcasting. Di Pietro is widely recognized for his devoted prayer life and zeal for revival. DiPietro, and his wife Melissa, moved to Kansas City to be near family and be a part of a global revival movement.

You can reach Di Pietro on his Facebook author page:
https://www.facebook.com/frankjjdipietro

Fiind out more about his books at:
TheResurgenceStore.com

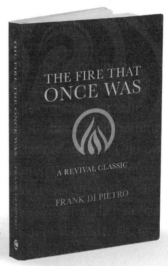

Also Available From Christos Publishing:

CARRIERS OF THE FIRE
VOLUMES 1-5

Each of these volumes feature the stories of devout, Spirit-led Christians from previous generations. The tales of old often enable us to experience a move of God afresh.

Fiind out more at TheResurgenceStore.com

Also Available From Christos Publishing:

THUNDER IN THE WHIRLWIND
A COLLECTION OF REVIVAL QUOTATIONS

"Your thunder roared from the whirlwind; the lightning lit up the world!
The earth trembled and shook" (Psalm 77:18).

This book is an inspiring collection of revival reflections. Read the personal insights of John Wesley, George Whitefield, Evan Roberts, Leonard Ravenhill, and a number of other firebrands.

This book will stir your heart and challenge you to seek the Lord afresh. Read *Thunder in the Whirlwind!*

Find out more at TheResurgenceStore.com

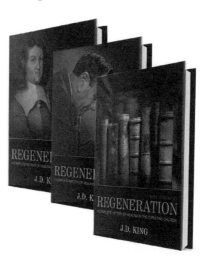

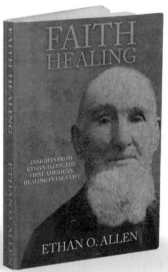

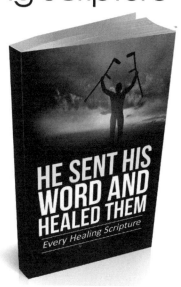

Also Available From Christos Publishing:

Healing in History
Series

The Healing in History Series by J.D. King is a multi-volume collection that explores the works of God through numerous Christian traditions. Be amazed at the wonderful stories of healing in multiple Christian traditions.

Find out more at TheResurgenceStore.com

Christos
Publishing